In Search of Environmental Excellence

Moving Beyond Blame

Bruce Piasecki
and Peter Asmus

Foreword by Jean-Michel Cousteau

Introduction by Congresswoman Claudine Schneider

Afterword by the Honorable Robert K. Dawson

A TOUCHSTONE BOOK
Published by Simon & Schuster Inc.
NEW YORK   LONDON   TORONTO   SYDNEY   TOKYO   SINGAPORE

Simon and Schuster/Touchstone
Simon & Schuster Building
Rockefeller Center
1230 Avenue of the Americas
New York, New York 10020

Designed by Sheree Goodman
Manufactured in the United States of America

10 9 8 7 6 5 4 3 2 1

10 9 8 7 6 5 4 3 2 1 Pbk.

Library of Congress Cataloging in Publication Data

Piasecki, Bruce, 1955–
    In search of environmental excellence : moving beyond blame /
    Bruce Piasecki and Peter Asmus ; Foreword by Jean-Michel Cousteau ;
    Introduction by Claudine Schneider ; Afterword by Robert K. Dawson.
        p.   cm.
    "A Touchstone book."
    Includes bibliographical references.
    1. Environmental protection—United States.   2. Economic
development–Environmental aspects—United States.   I. Asmus.
    Peter.   II. Title.
TD171.P53   1990
363.7'00973—dc20   90-10078
                                                                        CIP

ISBN 0-671-69089-2
ISBN 0-671-69090-6 Pbk.

*To Andrea Masters
and
Lori Ann Asmus*

Contents

Acknowledgments

Unlike a place of business, the opposite of a fortress, dissimilar to any factory floor, this book is a bridge of words that people can choose to cross.

At this moment in world history, we believe it useful to document the search for environmental excellence. Since World War II, industrial nations have pursued a path of growth and innovation which has become increasingly questioned because of its stubborn inattentiveness to environmental-management concerns. Can we continue to grow in population, resource use, and emissions? New York City already gives off eight times as much heat as it receives from the sun; Tokyo, Rome, and Bonn are not far behind. Is it possible to redesign modern manufacturing and transport so that we can produce the same products with less wastes, less energy, and fewer materials? What would a new, more environmentally benign industrialism look like?

We wrote this book, and built an excellent team of colleagues, to pursue some answers.

Bruce Piasecki would like to acknowledge Andrea Masters, who, once again, offered understanding and insight, and Chris Adelmann, who first pointed me in the direction of Simon and Schuster. Thanks also to Lettie Lee of the Ann Elmo Agency for her astute sense of the book market, and to Susan Poisson, Linda Champagne, and Howard Jack for their attentive responses to my lecture series at the New York State Museum based on the chapters of this book.

After two technical and legal books on environmental affairs, I wanted to write in color, to provide a commentary that might assemble rather than divide. My deepest thanks, then, to Peter Asmus. This has been a wonderful instance of what collaborative efforts can yield. Thanks, also, to my colleagues at the American Hazard Control Group, especially Chris Hynes, James Atkinson, Robin McClellan, and Monica Smith. As a consulting group, you are living proof that environmental management work makes sense.

Special thanks to Dr. Irvin White and his cast of eighty-five at the New York State Energy Research and Development Authority, especially Gunnar Walmet and Brad Hollomon. As a model public corporation, developing and diversifying energy supplies through co-funding, research, and development, NYSERDA gave me an institutional home while on this two-year leave from university teaching. They gave me much more: a brilliant set of colleagues, access to a state's empire of reports and statistics, as well as research funds. This book could not have happened without this generous support from NYSERDA.

Peter Asmus would like to acknowledge his wife, Lori Ann Asmus, whose faithful support through the lean years contributed to the development of this book in a big way.

The beauty of this book is that it is the product of so many sources of knowledge. Hats off to John Kirlin, editor of USC's *California Policy Choices,* an annual publication whose institutional support fostered a greater understanding of energy policy in California, as well as the development of the art of the discerning edit. Thanks also to Dan Tanz and the other editors at McGraw-Hill energy newsletters, for allowing room for energy reporting. Likewise, appreciation goes to Arthur O'Donnell of *California Energy Markets.* Many thanks to Charles Imbrecht and his California Energy Commission, an institution that proved to be a well of information, and to the University of California–Davis, whose conferences on global warming proved most useful for Chapter 3.

My deepest appreciation to the many newspapers, magazines, and foundation supporters over the years: especially authors

James Boyd and Taylor Branch, Dan Noyes with the Center for Investigative Reporting, and Bill Moore with the *Sacramento Bee*.

Finally, we would like to acknowledge Carole Hall, James Nichols, and André Bernard, our editors, who provided friendly expertise and useful comments page by page. Solid media advice came from Patricia Eisemann and her assistant Marcy A. Steinberg, also of Simon and Schuster, who proved their claim that "after authors make a book, we make it move."

Foreword

When my father began diving in the Mediterranean Sea in the early forties, the water was clean. Great beds of seagrass and algae thrived there, along with dense schools of fish and rich invertebrate fauna. Gorgonians were abundant, and so were huge groupers and spiny lobsters. It was the rich sea-floor community the world was seeing in the early Cousteau films.

Since those days, the Mediterranean coast has become densely populated. Industries, hotels, and homes line the coast. Sewage and other wastes stream into the sea. Sadly, the same waters where the first Aqua-lung divers discovered the sea's beauty and diversity are today biologically impoverished. And this scene— where urban development meets the water—is spreading rapidly around the world today.

I recall the reaction of Albert Falco, who has been a member of the Cousteau team for nearly forty years and was one of the earliest undersea pioneers. "Our magnificent natural aquarium," he said, "has been transformed into a large decanting basin, collecting the dregs of our life on land. To be sure, the water is still clear in the open sea ten miles offshore. But we don't go swimming in the middle of the ocean."

Since World War II, a flood of new technologies and products has been produced without innovations to avoid the accompanying new kinds of harmful waste products. Combined with growing human population needs, the productive ecosystems of the planet have become overburdened to the point where they are collapsing in many places. Our blind trust in nature, as Piasecki and Asmus note in this new book, has betrayed us. While there is a self-cleaning capacity in nature, scientists are now finding that this process can take generations, depending on the extent of the damage. If all pollution were halted today, for example, it could still take many, many years for the Baltic to recover.

During my travels around the world, our teams have witnessed many hopeless scenes—hopeless because people did not understand the dangers confronting them; they *did* have the tools to solve their predicament. When people band together, make coalitions, gather available information, and plot an effective strategy, mountains shrink into molehills. Impediments are overcome.

Years ago, the Cousteau Society was asked to participate with many other groups and individuals in a hearing in Brownsville, Texas, to evaluate the feasibility of burning at sea some of the most dangerous toxic wastes known to humanity. At first suspicious and uninformed about this technology, people joined efforts to question it. After talking with a variety of experts, including Bruce Piasecki, the Cousteau Society and fellow activists concluded there were safer land-based treatment alternatives that could cost-effectively take the place of at-sea burning.

In general, remedies exist for most of the ills that humanity visits upon marine, freshwater, and terrestrial systems. As my father stated in the early 1970s, "We must decide to prevent rather than cure. As far as industry is concerned, this means putting zero levels of toxic materials into the waters. The executives of an industry should be required to consume in their company cafeterias the same water being discharged from their factories into the environment." Piasecki's two previous books, *Beyond Dumping* (1984) and *America's Future in Toxic Waste Management* (1988), verify this approach. His new book with Peter Asmus goes even further in its scope, defining preventive strategies. The producer of toxic wastes should ultimately be responsible for destroying or detoxifying all wastes before any effluent leaves the confines of the production facility. Our proposal has always been to have industry bear one-third of the costs, the federal government one-third, and the regional community in which the industry is located one-third. For industry, the costs of environmental protection should be included in the cost of the product or service. We must be prepared to pay the real costs, including the hidden environmental ones, of our material goods. Were the United States and other industrial nations to have taken this stance and enforced it years ago, tens of billions of dollars of public money, perhaps ultimately hundreds of billions, which must be spent on cleanup, could have been saved and used for more productive purposes.

Whenever environmental protection is not calculated into the cost of goods, we force future generations to pay. And, as we are now discovering, the cost increases with time as environmental and public health problems multiply, placing growing burdens on our children. My own father has been active in the environmental movement for many years.

Today, humankind faces an uncertain future. Will the strategy to store nuclear wastes from nuclear-weapons production and nuclear power turn vast areas into what Bruce Piasecki calls "national sacrifice zones"? Will the inefficient use of petroleum and the concomitant inability of governments to encourage development of alternative energy sources and more efficient hydrocarbon technologies bring the present society, dependent on this nonrenewable and polluting fuel, to a sudden slowdown or chaotic halt? Will the hunger to cut the trees of the rain forest—whether for luxurious furniture, throwaway chopsticks, cardboard for packaging, or to clear grazing land—contribute to an alteration of the climate of the planet, degrading regional environments, wildlife, and societies? Will the storage and inefficient disposal of hazardous wastes contaminate freshwater sources and living organisms for generations to come?

These are among the issues contemplated and resolved in *In Search of Environmental Excellence*. The problems are vast; the fear they create is real. Yet, this book argues, the solutions for many of these problems are available today. The key is to go beyond the complex of fear and blame caused by inadequate information and inadequate cooperation between government (national, state, and local), industry, and community. Working together, we can overcome our problems, and the quality of life for future generations can be preserved. Such is the timely argument of this book, which excites as it educates.

Bruce Piasecki and Peter Asmus offer a ray of hope and a blue-print for solutions to the vast array of environmental challenges before us. The authors show how we as a global community have gone wrong; but they also argue that, by gathering together to share appropriate information and technology, we can learn to understand and to solve our environmental dilemma.

At the individual level, each of us can make small changes to affect these large problems. Start recycling, or recycle more. Use less water. Save energy. Insulate your home. In the net, we, as a species, can effect significant, earth-revitalizing changes.

It is easy to say to a polluter, "No, you can't manufacture this product in this manner with the accompanying pollution," yet offer no alternative approach. It is more difficult to say, "No, but how about this solution?" At the Cousteau Society, we use the second approach, and it has been shared by Piasecki, Asmus, and others in a new generation of environmental writers.

Despite society's best efforts to prevent disasters, they still oc-cur, as this book highlights—ranging from the environmental blunders of ancient Rome and Greece to Hanford and Chernobyl, to Valdez and Bhopal.

How we plan for the future will determine our success or fail-ure. Remarkably, there is no national or international agency in society whose primary concern is the future, although our deci-sions cast long shadows ahead. Consequently, we lurch through time, reacting to one emergency after another, trying to rectify problems rather than prevent them, consuming, despoiling, and eradicating the life-support system for our own progeny. We are borrowing from tomorrow's environmental bank accounts, and leaving damaging debts for our children to pay.

In Search of Environmental Excellence applies a new measure to our environmental dilemmas: that we must consider first and foremost how they will impact the unborn generations to come. We as a society must begin to act now as if in the very presence of those future generations whose planet we can plunder or preserve.

—Jean-Michel Cousteau
1990

Revitalizing America:
An Introduction

There is an ever-present temptation to succumb to the doom-and-gloom stories saturating the media. Without a doubt, the news of the past decade has been bleak concerning the environment. There are more malnourished people in the world than ever before. Since 1980, the arms race has diverted over $6 trillion from investments that could have spurred economic productivity and dramatically raised people's living standards.

Moreover, recent discovery of a Texas-size hole in the stratospheric ozone layer over Antarctica gives new urgency to the need to phase out ozone-depleting chemicals. Already, the ozone layer above Antarctica has declined by fifty percent. North America has experienced a three-percent decrease so far—triple the level predicted by previous scientific models. The world's best scientists estimate that each one-percent decline in the ozone layer leads to a two-percent increase in ultraviolet radiation, triggering a five-percent increase in skin cancers.

The 1980s saw more years of record-breaking high temperatures than any other decade over the past century. This trend conforms to what many scientists anticipate occurring, given the unchecked growth of infrared-trapping "greenhouse gas" emissions.

But the future is not fated; our destiny need not manifest itself as an unending series of costly and painful environmental disasters. There exists an abundance of viable alternative options, if we choose to take them.

That is what *In Search of Environmental Excellence* is all about: envisioning a far healthier, more prosperous, and more secure future than current management strategies will produce. Bruce Piasecki and Peter Asmus exemplify the kind of active rethinking of environmental management challenges that we all must undertake if we are to "renew America" and, by example, offer a model by which other nations can glean the elements of renewal appropriate to their own unique cultural, environmental, political, and economic conditions. This book is about revitalization in the broadest, most global sense.

The authors' fundamental message is one that needs to be heard far and wide, over and over again: Economic vitality need not, and should not, be pursued at the expense of environmental quality. Destroying or deteriorating the quality of our air, water, soils, forests, and other natural resources will exact huge costs sooner or later.

As the advancing science of ecology is teaching us, natural resources are not infinitely resilient and sustainable. This book outlines what a sensible estimate of nature would look like. As we approach or exceed these limits we pay for our deeds, one way or another. Acid rain, for example, causes respiratory ailments, erodes buildings, collapses the fish populations in thousands of lakes, reduces the resistance of forests to attacks by pests and pathogens, and destroys over $10 billion per year in U.S. economic benefits. Improperly disposed hazardous wastes, Piasecki has shown in his previous two books, contaminate community water systems, cause increased cancer in downwind populations, and force expensive relocations of neighborhoods or entire communities.

Piasecki and Asmus have done a consummate job of scanning the globe for success stories of how adversities have been or are being transformed into advantages. Where they found crises, they also have found innovations. Mountains of solid wastes with nowhere to be dumped have given rise to comprehensive recycling and composting programs in Europe and Japan. Corporate hazardous waste programs like the 3M Company's are cutting hazardous waste in half and saving hundreds of millions of dollars in the process.

America needs a new orientation, a new kind of environmental management, that stresses preventive measures over crisis management. As the authors note, America's thirty thousand Love Canals and scores of severely contaminated weapons production facilities, with their $300 billion cleanup bill, have taught us a harsh lesson: If the real costs of polluting had been factored in from the start, America would not be facing these environmental deficit challenges since it would have made good business sense to operate in an environmentally benign fashion.

It is this preventive strategy that I believe will work well in the Congress. More and more members of Congress now know that foresight is cheaper than hindsight. As this book details at length, the achievement of a high quality of life does not require us to exhaust or pollute natural resources. More often than not, human ingenuity and innovation can deliver us the goods and services we need and desire while reducing both costs and pollutants.

Consider just one example, which I have been promoting this past decade in Congress: using energy more efficiently and renewably. Energy is the lifeblood of the global economy. We can't live without it, yet we are causing numerous problems with it. Currently, most of the world's energy comes from depletable resources like coal, oil, gas, and uranium. Half of the world's oil has already been burned, and many of the remaining deposits occur in environmentally fragile areas like the Arctic National Wildlife Refuge. Not only drilling, but shipping this oil can be damaging, as dramatically evidenced by Exxon's wrecked oil tanker *Valdez* in Alaska's pristine Prince William Sound.

Fossil-fuel use is a culprit in acid rain, urban smog, and the warming of the global atmosphere, the so-called greenhouse effect. Nuclear power, while not contributing to any of these crises, is beset with its own problems: accidents like Three Mile Island and Chernobyl; the vulnerability of plants as targets of military planners, terrorists and saboteurs; and the production of radioactive wastes that must be guarded for millennia.

Despite these and numerous other energy-related dilemmas, conventional energy projections call for a two- to fourfold increase in energy consumption over the next fifty years. Even a doubling of energy would require all of the following: bringing on-line the equivalent of an Alaskan pipeline every other month, a 1,000-megawatt coal plant every other day, and a 1,000-megawatt nuclear plant every four days, and doubling OPEC's output to maximum capacity. The environmental and social impacts would be equally daunting. Carbon emissions from the burning of fossil fuels would triple, worsening the greenhouse effect, acid rain, and urban ozone. Finally, the costs of such an energy future are staggering. Developing countries, already debt-strapped and economically depressed, would have to increase export earnings fifteen percent per year beyond inflation.

Conventional energy forecasts imply that this dire future is inevitable, if we are to accommodate a doubling of world population and a quadrupling of gross work product. End of story? Not by a long shot. In the final half of *In Search of Environmental Excellence,* Piasecki and Asmus outline the likely answers. In describing what the global-warming challenge means to the industrialized world, they suggest ways for us to get off the "petrochemical treadmill." They offer a solid, readable summary of what better environmental management would look like, as well as clever accounts on how our homes, cars, and backyards are part of the answer.

Piasecki has done this kind of future planning before, especially in his two books on hazardous-waste management. With co-author Gary Davis he established the need to look abroad for environmental answers. While U.S. industry has been slow to recognize the cash value of prevention, industry elsewhere is making rapid progress. Companies in France, Denmark, the Netherlands, and the Federal Republic of Germany are finding that the equipment and processes they developed to reduce waste are not only cutting production and disposal costs, but have become valuable products in themselves in a growing world market for "clean technology."

In *America's Future in Toxic Waste Management: Lessons from Europe* (1988), Piasecki and Davis isolated four reasons for Europe's early lead in waste-reduction technology: the scarcity of remote sites for land disposal; fear of contaminating groundwater, a common source of drinking water in Europe; memories of post-World War II material scarcity, which gave rise to a strong conservation ethic and recycling practices; and a traditionally high level of cooperation between government and industry. With their options so limited, European companies had no choice but to redesign products and production processes to reduce hazardous-waste production. Today, the same approach is necessary in America, and many of us in Congress are pressing for such preventive strategies.

A few quick examples Davis and Piasecki brought us from France serve to make the point: Government has a legitimate role in providing more efficient environmental-management and energy systems. In France, many new "clean " technologies are being researched, developed, demonstrated, and commercialized through government-funded programs. In 1979, the French government set up the Mission for Clean Technologies, which provides grants of up to ten percent of project costs for innovative approaches that can be used by all companies producing a specific product. Another French agency, the Research Service, provides grants of up to fifty percent for research on clean technologies that apply to a whole range of products. The French tax code, moreover, allows for rapid depreciation of pollution-prevention investments. Industries may write off fifty percent of the capital costs of a waste-reduction project during the first year of operation.

Many improvements resulted from decisions made by millions of individuals to purchase more fuel-efficient cars, insulate their homes, and install high-efficiency appliances. Similar benefits could result from the reform agenda proposed in *In Search of Environmental Excellence*. The message is now more timely and more global in its applications. Never before in history have individual actions come to play so profound a role, for good and ill, on the course of world events. Prevention pays, and it is incumbent upon each and every one of us to capitalize upon resource-conserving and pollution-reducing opportunities.

We owe Bruce Piasecki and Peter Asmus a debt of gratitude for preparing such a rich resource guide, showing how each of us can renew America through our own actions, and the actions we should demand from our elected and appointed policymakers.

—Congresswoman Claudine Schneider
1990

Prologue:
Setting the Course
for a Better Way

On October 14, 1974, a ship named the *Vulcanus* paused 165 miles southwest of Galveston, Texas, in the Gulf of Mexico. Its toxic cargo consisted of obsolete military wastes, spent petrochemical residues, and small quantities of dreaded hazards such as DDT, Agent Orange, and related chlorinated hydrocarbons. The crew prepared its two giant kilns for the first experimental burn off the U.S. coast.

The burn—a process referred to as ocean incineration—was considered a critical success. Since World War II, mountains of toxic liquid had been stockpiled; incidents such as the disaster at Love Canal were beginning to show the world how badly landfills leak, and everyone was looking for an out. Three more test burns were carried out in 1974 alone. Yet attempts to monitor the effectiveness of the burns remained riddled with uncertainties.

Eleven years later, I was asked to testify against ocean incineration in Brownsville, Texas. The largest hearing hall in the port city was packed with concerned spectators, including local cattle ranchers, citrus farmers, and shrimp fishermen. Outside the hearing room, several thousand more protesters chanted, "No more burns."

Having researched the effects of incineration in Europe, I was called on to describe the safer alternatives that German officials had discovered for the same troubling wastes. This, I felt, was particularly significant new evidence, since the Germans had initiated ocean burns. After twenty years of experience in the North Sea, they must have wanted to stop it for good reasons.

During the recess, two six-foot men, both dressed in suits and cowboy boots, approached me outside the hearing room. Fixing his tie, the taller fellow said, "Dr. Piasecki, you are on the wrong side."

"Let's be real," the other man interjected, "America needs to do something with these stockpiled wastes. No one is letting them burn toxics on land. Ocean burning is the only way to go."

"Perhaps," I suggested, "we should pursue your concerns in a friendlier setting." Resuming our conversation in a nearby bar, we spent several hours in disagreement before they revealed themselves as representatives from the firm seeking the Brownsville permit. Chemical Waste Management, the world's largest waste handler, was losing several thousand dollars a week to service their loans as the ship awaited the permits. "And," the taller one added, "every month we don't burn, folks like you are causing more cancer."

The Environmental Protection Agency inched closer and closer to sanctioning ocean incineration from 1985 to 1987. With the direct support of President Reagan, hundreds of millions were being spent by the Maritime Administration to build a fleet of vessels. Wall Street analysts anticipated the eventual market for ocean incineration to exceed two billion dollars per year by 1990.

During those same years, however, a remarkable opposition took shape. In 1987, seven high school teachers, calling themselves the Gulf Coast Coalition for Public Health (GCCPH), delivered thirteen thousand signatures directly to the EPA administrator. "We let them know that we meant business," recalls GCCPH's science coordinator Jackie Lockett, "and if they are going to grant permits to burn off Texas, they best also grant Pacific and Atlantic permits."

Suddenly, the war was spreading, and battles formed on three distinct fronts: in the Gulf, off the New Jersey coast, and in a harbor near San Francisco's Fisherman's Wharf. Seemingly overnight, ocean incineration became a national concern.

During 1987, I was enlisted to testify in San Francisco, armed with the latest European complaints about dumped vessel ash, chronic loading spills, and the inadequate policing of the burns in the North Sea. No longer convinced that the approach was safe, the Dutch had even commissioned a monitoring plane to follow their ships. Several more attempted burns took place in the North Sea. Despite temperatures reaching 1,800° Fahrenheit, the smoke—a telltale sign of incomplete combustion—continued to belch out of the kilns.

While still out West, I was interviewed by Peter Asmus on the issue. He was digging deeper and deeper into the silent corporate interests advocating the ocean burns. I thought to myself at the time, "He is asking the right questions, and wants to be part of the answer." His resulting lead story in *Greenpeace* magazine highlighted my research on European waste-management innovations to show citizens that there were cleaner, safer alternatives. During the same period, the White House and the EPA reversed themselves on ocean incineration.

The ocean incineration issue brought us, and many others like us, together, and we shared in the victory. Federal budget restraints ultimately dealt the final crushing blow to the program, but its defeat really occurred because the public now knew there was a better way.

In the future, solutions to the most far-reaching environmental dilemmas must come from private citizens as well as from industry and the government. Environmentally conscious choices by individuals may seem insignificant when viewed alone, but collectively they can fuel desperately needed changes.

The goal of this book is to articulate the new set of reliable alternatives available to us, and to further the momentum toward excellence already initiated by thousands of specialists, entrepreneurs, and citizens. During our research we have uncovered many examples of environmental excellence. With each new discovery, certain patterns and principles resurfaced again and again. Armed with a knowledge of these principles, each one of us can shatter the myths of our industrial past and, in the process, offer hope to a world groping for answers.

—Bruce Piasecki
1990

In Search of Environmental Excellence

Part One

Past Mistakes

Chapter 1

Taking Stock:
Whatever Happened to the
Grand Old Earth?

Man strides over the earth, and deserts follow in his footsteps.

—*Ancient Proverb*

The earth does not argue,
Is not pathetic, has no arrangements,
Does not scream, haste, persuade, threaten, promise.
Makes no discriminations, has no conceivable failures,
Closes nothing, refuses nothing, shuts none out,
Of all powers, objects, states, it notifies,
  shuts none out.

—*Walt Whitman*
"Song of the Rolling Earth"

Americans, without acknowledging it, worship the resilience of nature. This blind trust in the ability of the earth to absorb the growing burden of man-made pollutants has cost us dearly.

Our disregard for the frailty of already stressed ecosystems has firm historical roots. Our collective consciousness has been defined by the likes of Walt Whitman, whose "Song of the Rolling Earth," written in the 1860s, sums up the depth of our trust in nature. Today these words reveal the seductive naïveté behind America's prevailing estimate of what nature can, and cannot, do.

These beliefs remain an active part of the American mindset.[1] They continue to color our response to environmental concerns, instructing us to repeat the pattern of our past mistakes. The most startling example is the state of our nuclear-weapons production sites. Our government has conceded that enormous tracts of land will be sealed off from the American people, perhaps for centuries. These lands are becoming known as "national sacrifice zones," and remind us of a longstanding debt we all share.

In trusting nature to absorb the by-products of nuclear-weapons production, we are finding out just how wrongheaded the old exuberance is. From the Savannah River Plant in South Carolina to the Hanford Reservation in Washington State, thousands of radioactive sites across the nation await remediation.

The notion that nature will absorb all industrial disruptions comfortably is dangerously entrenched in American life.[2] America's innocent appraisal of nature has a rich history; its clearest articulation occurred roughly one hundred years ago.

A young, vital America was experiencing tremendous material advances. Unexpected and magnificent mineral treasures became opened with the colonization of Texas, the acquisition of Oregon, and the occupation of the Southwest along the Santa Fe Trail. An explosion in railroad-, steamship-, and canal-building was encouraged by the promise of unbounded profits and cheap energy. With accessible coal and oil in Pennsylvania, lead throughout the Midwest, copper by Lake Superior, and the discovery of gold in California, our expanding economy's consumption of the nation's supply of resources appeared to make divine sense.

Starry-eyed entrepreneurs reveled in the unparalleled growth America's economy achieved. "Texas," a common nineteenth-century slogan read, "can feed the world."

Along with these economic miracles, the United States began inheriting the unfortunate by-products of environmental neglect. In 1880 alone, gold-crazed speculators washed 53.5 million cubic yards of debris into once-pristine California rivers. Still, the smoke of industrial stacks in New York and Boston, in Erie and Chicago, was welcomed as a sign of economic prosperity, not seen as a cause for concern.

Today, toxic landfills, global warming, and oil spills show that wealth based on fossil fuels and wasteful technologies is short-changing the future. Our lands, water, and air now demand far better, more effective management if we are to survive. At fault, of course, is no single individual or cast of sinister characters, but a pattern of consumer and corporate decision-making that has misread and ignored the limits of nature's capacity to assimilate human footprints.

This pattern is a subtle one, which has repeated itself throughout history. It is a pattern that demonstrates nature's need for a proper ratio between preservation and use. Industrial societies can no longer stubbornly refuse to acknowledge these natural needs. We must not forget that a recurring pattern of environmental abuse has played a major role in prompting the decline of many great civilizations.

The Patterns of Environmental Abuse

We have to travel back to Greek and Roman civilizations to appreciate fully the evolution of government in world society and its increasingly difficult task of protecting its citizens from environmental tragedies. The Greeks were among the first to inflict long-lasting scars on the earth.

Historians and tourists alike consider the ruins of the Parthenon an enduring symbol of the grandeur of Greek civilization. But the bare, desolate surrounding mountains are also monuments to an ecological disaster brought on by the Greeks. Once, almost half of Greece was forested. But trees were used to fuel the Greek democracy, and a massive deforestation—which occurred primarily between 600 and 200 B.C.—stripped the land. Eventually, because of the need for lumber to build ships, the Greeks began to require replanting in some cases. There was no consistency in government policy, however. In the fourth century B.C. in the city of Cyprus, kings carefully conserved trees. But by the next century, rulers offered incentives, such as title to the property, for those who ruthlessly harvested forests.

The most damaging activities of Greece, however, were its overgrazing practices. Domestic animals, such as goats, permanently denuded thousands of square miles of Mediterranean hillsides. Once the vegetation was gone, widespread erosion swept the land, completing the devastation. Today, less than a tenth of the land mass has trees. Though Greek agricultural practices were advanced for their time and introduced some new conservation techniques, the dwindling resource base, coupled with population pressures, expedited the decline of that remarkable civilization.

The Romans followed Greek practices, but because of the size of their conquests and the consumptive appetite of their ruling class, Rome's destructive and mindless exploitation of resources was even more damaging. Deforestation was again a primary problem, causing further erosion and widespread flooding, but the Romans also found several new ways to abuse their environment. Perhaps the most distressing aspect of the Roman Empire was its decimation of wildlife. At the dedication of the Colosseum under Titus, for instance, nine thousand animals were slaughtered in one hundred days. Trajan's conquest over Dacia was celebrated by the destruction of eleven thousand animals. An entire entertainment industry—an ancient Hollywood—fed off of such excesses. Huge canals were constructed to steer the flow of blood into the fields, some of which, according to French annals, stank until the Middle Ages. Such gruesome practices contributed to the extinction of the rhinoceros, elephant, and zebra in North Africa.

Roman mining practices accelerated soil erosion and introduced heavy metals, particularly lead, into the water supplies. Though some writers at the time postulated that soils were in decline because of overuse, government policies ignored this fact. Irrigation systems, while impressive for their time, failed to take into account the detrimental effects of accumulating deposits and silting on navigable waters.

The Roman and Greek examples typify the failures of past governments to protect citizens from an overemphasis on immediate use of resources. Rather than encouraging more efficient practices and fostering the idea of strategic reserves, they lived for the day, making themselves vulnerable. If Greece and Rome, considered among the greatest civilizations of their times, could not effectively balance the needs of their societies with ecological prudence, what will happen to the United States in today's rapidly changing world? Our environmental challenges are far more complicated than those faced by these ancient civilizations; our continued survival requires dramatic responses to the recurrent pattern of abuse.

Our Lands

Historians agree that the three worst environmental calamities in world history have occurred on land. These are the deforestation of China's uplands, which sabotaged food and water supplies about 3000 B.C.; the aforementioned destruction of fertile lands in the Mediterranean region by the Greeks and Romans; and America's contribution, the Dust Bowl of the 1930s.

In America's heartland, the Midwest, years of shortsighted agricultural practices suddenly caught up with us. The droughts and heat of the summer of 1934, with temperatures consistently over 100° F., killed 370 people in the state of Illinois. Devastating dust storms in 1935 carried away more than twice the tonnage of soil that was scooped out to make the Panama Canal. By 1936, farm losses reached $25 million a day.

The inorganic content of the dust in those storms contained as much risk to the public as lead. Today, we would have even more to worry about. Given decades of chemical misuse and the ever-increasing concentrations of toxins, pesticides, and herbicides introduced into the nation's heartland during the last half century, future dust storms might create contaminated clouds that could poisonously infest whole communities.

The mindset that created the Dust Bowl—an event only fifty years in the making—is vividly captured by America's celebrated environmental historian, Donald Worster, in his book, *Dust Bowl.* "Americans blazed their way across a richly endowed continent with a ruthless, devastating efficiency unmatched by any people anywhere," Worster wrote. "When the white men came to the plains, they talked expansively of busting and breaking the land. And that is exactly what they did. Some environmental catastrophes are nature's work, others are the slowly accumulating effects of ignorance or poverty. The Dust Bowl, in contrast, was the inevitable outcome of a culture that deliberately, self-consciously, set itself that task of dominating and exploiting the land for all it was worth."

Today, much of the 97-million acre area marred by the Dust Bowl has a permanent disfiguration. The transformation of those once pristine fields into dust should stand as a lasting reminder that nature cannot always compensate for the excesses of civilization. Unfortunately, it appears that the lessons of the Dust Bowl have not been adequately learned.

As the dust began to settle in the mid to late 1930s, the states that had been devastated began groping for solutions. Some successes in replanting native and imported grasses had convinced administrators that the right tools and crops were all the southern Great Plains needed. Salvation would come from technology, not from a reorientation of business practices or a fundamental change in farming procedures.

Many people agreed on the need to replant the grasses that would prevent such widespread destruction, but the practical difficulties of convincing thousands of farmers to plant their share of grasses without seeing an immediate return on their investment doomed the full-scale program originally envisioned. The Soil Conservation and Domestic Allotment Act of 1936 paid farmers to leave some of their land fallow, but it only lasted two years. Government purchases of land helped to promote some progress on this front, but finally cash crops once again displaced these grasses to turn the desert temporarily green again.

Hopes of drastic agricultural reform faded as the rain's return helped agricultural production surpass even the good times of earlier years. Bigger and better machines, federal price supports, and the adoption of some conservation measures began the whole destructive cycle all over again. By the end of World War II, wheatfields in sixty-nine southern plains counties had expanded by 2.5 million acres, and the sandy dune areas replanted at federal expense were rejuvenated, but were then quickly replowed at rates much faster than pre–Dust Bowl averages.

Conservation basics, such as contour plowing and fallowing, were adopted to some extent, but were often sacrificed if some new machine or method promised faster and larger profits. Conservation techniques were not viewed as valuable in and of themselves; instead, they were seen within the context of the expanding appetite of a first-class world power. The fundamental truth is that the Dust Bowl was not the result of the wrath of nature, but a direct result of human intervention.

Without the guiding hand of an enlightened government utiliz-

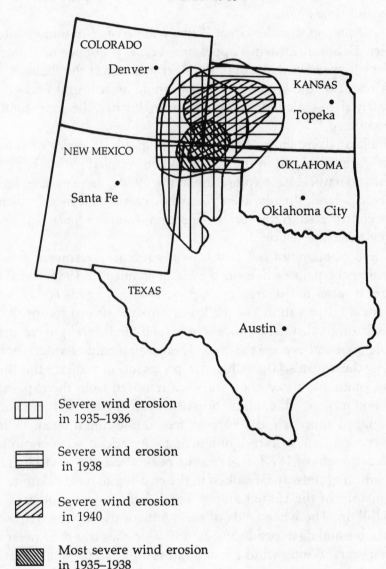

WHERE THE DUST BOWL HIT
1935–1940

COLORADO
Denver •

KANSAS
• Topeka

NEW MEXICO

• Santa Fe

OKLAHOMA

• Oklahoma City

TEXAS

Austin •

Severe wind erosion
in 1935–1936

Severe wind erosion
in 1938

Severe wind erosion
in 1940

Most severe wind erosion
in 1935–1938

Source: **Donald Worster,** *Dust Bowl*

ing its resources to protect the long-term resource needs of a nation, such large-scale environmental abuses repeat themselves time and time again.

Some predict that the Great Plains will become an unpopulated desert. Deborah Epstein Popper and Frank J. Popper of Rutgers University predict that "over the next generation the Plains will, as a result of the largest, longest-running agricultural and environmental miscalculation in American history, become totally depopulated."[3]

Their analysis shows how the boom-and-bust cycles of subsidized farming began in the 1930s. When coupled with the cycles of oil and natural-gas exploration in the 1970s, these policies have ravaged a land already deeply scarred. Past government policies have contributed to the current dilemma; future policies will have to revitalize the region.

The Poppers point out that the only recent government policy soothing the pain of lives in the Great Plains is a 1985 law that makes it easier to declare bankruptcy. They have gone so far as to call for a "deprivation" of the lower Great Plains to return them to their original state, a process by which the federal government would own and oversee the land. Their plan would establish in the region the world's largest historic preservation project: the Buffalo Commons, a vast shortgrass sea removed from the exploitation and misguided manipulation of its recent past. Without such a managed approach, the Poppers feel, the southern Great Plains will remain "an austere monument to American self-delusion."

The drought of 1988, which at its peak affected close to half of the nation's landscape, resulted in the costliest natural calamity in the history of the United States. Total damage was estimated at $39 billion. The wheatfields of the southern plains were reduced to stubble and dust, producing a 1989 yield that was the lowest in eleven years. Winter wind-erosion rates surpassed the highest rates of the last three decades and approached Dust Bowl levels; 4.8 million acres of Kansas topsoil blew away on one day in March 1989. Yet we soon forget these facts with the renewal of rain, just as we forget the lessons learned from Greece and Rome.

Other countries, however, have taken a fresh look at the past to answer some current land-use problems. A reintroduction of farming techniques used three thousand years ago high in the Peruvian Andes, for example, is now being heralded as a possible solution to many of the economic and environmental woes of developing nations.

In these farming methods, abandoned in the sixteenth century but now replicated by archaeologists, raised platforms are planted with crops which, in turn, are irrigated by canals that cross-stitch the fields. The success of this technique has been so superior to that of the so-called Green Revolution, with its reliance on chemicals and machinery, that the Peruvian experiment is now being hailed as an environmentally benign, low-cost way to increase developing countries' agricultural yields dramatically in locations characterized by harsh conditions and limited financial resources. This method withstands both drought and flooding better than conventional high-tech farming techniques. A breakthrough such as this illustrates the axiom that less is often more, and offers hope that we can, after all, learn from the past.

Our Waters

The Great Lakes—Superior, Michigan, Huron, Erie, and Ontario—collectively span more than 750 miles from east to west with a surface area exceeding 94,000 square miles. They constitute the largest system of fresh surface water on earth, containing eighteen percent of the total world supply. Only the polar ice caps contain more.

The astonishing magnitude of the Great Lakes makes it difficult to appreciate their equally astonishing fragility. For centuries, it was thought that such a vast expanse could absorb, and neutralize, anything. Yet despite their size, the Great Lakes are highly vulnerable to pollutants.

It would be naïve to claim that the current toxic threat to the Great Lakes was anticipated. Throughout the nineteenth century, and well into this century, wastes from steel and paper mills and chemicals from factories were dumped directly into waterways that flow into the lakes. It would also be dishonest to say that the repercussions from environmental abuses in the region are new. In 1854, five percent of Chicago's population died due to a cholera epidemic. By 1891, 124 out of every 100,000 Chicago deaths were attributed to typhoid.[4] In response, cities hurried to protect drinking water from urban wastes. Chicago actually reversed the flow of the Chicago River in an attempt to free Lake Michigan of the sewage.

Most public-works projects undertaken in the Great Lakes since 1850 have been attempts at environmental management of pollutants. The sources of pollution are numerous. Today, residual toxins arrive from throughout most of North America. Since nearly twenty-five percent of Canada's and seven percent of the United States' total agricultural production surrounds the freshwater basin, farm chemicals are a common local irritant. In addition, urban waste continues to be a major source of pollution to the lakes: one-quarter of all Canadians and a tenth of all Americans live in the region, and the volume of waste is staggering. The steel industry is also clustered around the lakes near Detroit and Cleveland. The low costs of water transportation prompted the development of iron ore, coal, and limestone mining, as well as the positioning of mills, near the lakes. Ore is shipped from mines near Lake Superior—the northernmost and most pristine lake—to steel mills at the south end of Lake Michigan.

Then there are the paper mills. Dense concentrations of them line Wisconsin's Fox River, which feeds into Lake Michigan's Green Bay. Chemical manufacturers, too, have developed both sides of the Niagara River because of the cheap electricity derived from dams.

The most haunting of human affronts to the area, however, is the discharge of synthetic organic chemicals and heavy metals into the lakes. Unlike other forms of pollution, these discharges can be acutely poisonous in very small amounts. Long-term exposure increases the risk of cancer, birth defects, and genetic mutations. Fish and wildlife that previously thrived in the Great Lakes are showing increasing signs of toxic contamination and stress. Cormorants are now sometimes born with crossed bills, making it impossible for them to eat and survive. Tumors are now not uncommon in several species of fish, including the sauger, and fewer fishermen than ever are eating what they catch.

According to public health authorities in New York and Canada, eating fish from the Great Lakes is far more dangerous than drinking or swimming in the polluted waters. A person who eats one meal of lake trout from Lake Michigan will be exposed to more PCBs than those accumulated over an entire lifetime of drinking the water. Although scientific research regarding the danger of eating contaminated food is still in its infancy, some distressing facts have already emerged. Mothers who eat fish from the lakes have higher concentrations of cancer-causing PCBs in their bodies and breast milk than those who don't.[5]

What can be done? As early as 1978, toxic contaminants had become the focus of concern in all Great Lakes water-quality agreements between the U.S. and Canada. In addition, in 1985 both the Royal Society of Canada and the U.S. National Academy of Sciences urged both governments to strengthen their controls of toxic emissions. The institutional response to these warnings has been slow, but change is nonetheless happening.

The scientific community has isolated the most dangerously polluted places. The International Joint Commission (IJC) has mapped out forty-two areas in the Great Lakes that require urgent help. Areas surrounding these hazardous spots now have strict limits on drinking, fishing, and swimming, and are being monitored by scientists, elected officials, and citizen groups through remedial action plans (RAPs).[6] The purpose of a RAP is to encourage jurisdictions to rehabilitate their own acute problems. RAP committees most often consist of twenty to thirty members representing a broad spectrum of interests, including industry as well as individual citizens. The effort is part of a new trend seeking consensus-building tools to forge well-integrated responses to toxic threats. When former enemies sit down face to face, they often come to realize that both sides have points of view that need to be considered. What might once have been used as a good opportunity for an exchange of no-holds-barred attacks evolves into a cooperative exercise whereby a variety of interests learn to trust and respect each other's real and different needs.

Most of the forty-two hot spots already identified are near the mouths of tributaries where active cities and industries have been situated, and contain contaminated sediments. Often such an area reveals evidence of major past mistakes, such as the use of banned or restricted materials such as DDT, PCBs, Mirex, and mercury.

Elaborate cleanup laws have often been ignored, or prove to be ineffective in stemming the tide of toxic industrial releases. The responsibility for rectifying the damage often falls on the shoulders of individuals, who can move boldly to go beyond the nation's existing regulations and laws and seek superior on-site waste management.

In the case of the Massena-Cornwall RAP, company executives from Alcoa, Reynolds, and an obsolete General Motors Foundry sat across from citizen activists, environmental attorneys, and scientists. In addition, Native Americans from the Saint Regis Mohawk Reservation expressed their own unique concerns. The search for an adequate cleanup plan takes years, and thus demands wide-ranging efforts from such a broad spectrum of problem solvers.

Right now, as they probably will do well into the late 1990s, hundreds of such community members are meeting to write their own RAPs. Their efforts are open to the public, and in communities throughout the Great Lakes region, thousands of citizens are becoming a part of the answer.

Our Air

The Eastman Kodak Company of Rochester, New York, is the nation's largest emitter of poisons into our air. Annually, the facility spits out close to 9 million pounds of methylene chloride alone. Methylene chloride is the most common U.S. air pollutant and has been classified as a "probable human carcinogen" by the EPA. Yet it enjoys widespread industrial use as a metals degreaser and paint remover.

There are at least thirty United States industrial plants that individually spew over 1 million pounds of poison into the air every year. But "the dirty thirty" are only part of the story. All told, according to an Environmental Protection Agency report, more than 2.7 billion pounds of toxics are released into the atmosphere each year. All of these releases are quite legal. Pollution has continued unabated because it was thought necessary for economic growth.[7]

The 1,600 statues and monuments which dot the 4,000-acre Gettysburg National Military Park in Pennsylvania are slowly dissolving. Landmarks such as the memorial at Cemetery Hill have been so badly eroded that letters can no longer be made out. The facial features of Lincoln giving his famous address, as well as those of the surrounding soldiers, are now worn smooth. The culprit is acid rain, a result of sulfur dioxide emissions from coal-burning plants and from millions of automobiles. Many of the largest of these plants operate in the Rust Belt, America's industrial midsection.

"It's a disastrous combination when you've got more monuments than anybody else and more acid rain than anybody else," says David Ballard, a Pennsylvania state park service director. "The damage has been particularly serious over the past ten years, and it's getting even worse. We've got to do something."

The Keystone State, which has the nation's worst acid rain, is an extreme example. Yet there is an important warning implicit in recognizing that our past industrial practices are eating away at our history. These practices may devour our future.

Not only are our monuments eroding, our great national parks are also fading from view. Vistas such as the Grand Canyon, with its regal rainbow of natural history, are obscured by smog from distant Los Angeles cars some 555 miles away, and by the sulfur dioxide releases from the three stacks of the gigantic Navajo Generating Station, located just 12 miles from the northern edge of Grand Canyon National Park. Former interior secretary Walter J. Hickel had noble words for the canyon. "It would be unthinkable for us to pollute it ourselves," he proclaimed. Today, the unthinkable has occurred, and a national treasure is in jeopardy.

Every winter, a disturbing haze descends upon the Grand Canyon, and the EPA claims the Navajo station is the most guilty party. The EPA wants to reduce the plant's emissions by ninety percent, an upgrade with a price tag as high as a billion dollars. Ironically, taxpayers will foot part of this bill, for the plant's owners include the U.S. Department of the Interior's Bureau of Reclamation.

The primary owner of the plant—the Salt River Project—has known for at least seven years that the plant could not comply with state emission standards, and has finally been persuaded to regularly test the plant's emissions. The Bureau of Reclamation, along with the Salt River Project and other Navajo plant owners, still argue that the methods of monitoring air pollution by the EPA are faulty. They claim that the Grand Canyon has always had haze. They don't feel they should be singled out to pay for the installation of scrubbers—pollution equipment to reduce emissions. After all, they already have invested $639 million in a plant where a third of the budget went to environmental technologies such as electrostatic ash precipitators, plant water recyclers, and local revegetation projects.

The debate over who is to blame for the blanket of pollutants that wraps itself around many of the country's landmarks, including the Grand Canyon, is a sobering display of how the search for excellence in the 1990s will often involve the air we breathe.

While many of our initial efforts to clean up the air have been focused on industrial sources of pollution, future efforts must also target mobile sources, and the activities of individuals. This shift is most evident in Los Angeles, home of the nation's deadliest air.

Asthma among Los Angeles children between the ages of six and eleven jumped fifty-eight percent in the 1970s. This increase is primarily due to the smog that settles not just over Los Angeles, but also eastward to the San Gorgonio Mountains and south to the sandy beaches of San Diego. "You could completely turn off all of San Diego, and there would still be days when this county violates ozone standards because of L.A.," reports Richard J. Smith of the San Diego County Air Pollution Control District.

Area doctors attributed a twenty-three-percent rise in asthma-related deaths in a four-county region in Southern California between 1980 and 1985 to the ever-present brown haze. Typically, a Los Angeleno will spend sixteen days out of every year coughing, suffering from a sore throat, or experiencing nausea because of smog.

For these conditions to improve, the freeway culture, which has epitomized Los Angeles since the 1950s, will have to be replaced by mass transit and by the consolidation of residential and commercial communities. These new neighborhoods will bring walking to and from work back into fashion. The freewheeling culture of Los Angeles will be challenged by the environmentally conscious lifestyle of the nineties.

A special government group—the South Coast Air Quality Management District—has been set up and given unprecedented powers to regulate lifestyles, industry practices, and future development. This agency has already established rules for the backyard barbecue which has become so much a part of our culture. New lighter fluids, as well as rules governing the number of days one can pull out the grill, speak to how severe the pollution problem is.

New tough rules being mandated by a state agency—the Air Resources Board—will slash the hydrocarbon emissions of today's cars in half, with the result that California's cars will be the cleanest in the nation.

Along with reductions in pollutants emitted from conventional vehicles, Los Angeles will also be the testing ground for a whole new generation of cars that run on fuels such as methanol—currently used in race cars—as well as on batteries charged up by power plants and, later, on futuristic hydrogen fuel cells. Already the City of Los Angeles has purchased ten thousand electric vehicles and thousands of cars that can run on methanol, ethanol, or natural gas.

When it comes to answering our air's problems, everyone must get involved. The business sector will have to develop new air-pollution control technologies, better manufacturing designs, and still more efficient cars. Government must enact and enforce laws that promote cleaner air. None of these efforts will be effective without the vigilance and support of citizens.

Government and Citizens Have a Role

In the last forty years, American industry has become so insistently wasteful in its exploitation of energy and natural resources that we appear to some as victims of a senile capitalism,[8] a mode of market manipulation whereby our emphasis on immediate use overrides the long-term profitability of managed preservation. We approach manufacturing as we approached farming in the Dust Bowl, pressing for today's yield at the expense of tomorrow, drawing on our reserves well beyond the level of present income.

A primary example of capitalism gone somewhat senile is the leveraged-buyout craze that has engulfed the nation. The rash of corporate takeovers not only reinforces the American industrial sector's preoccupation with the short-term balance sheet, but also undermines the sustained commitment to R&D projects that might otherwise lead to the discovery of environmentally benign solutions to manufacturing challenges. "Longer-range R&D is not being supported as strongly as it used to be because of the push to enhance shareholder value and stock prices," warns Charles Larson, executive director of the Industrial Research Institute. "It may have a severe impact on our long-range competitiveness." We seem to have forgotten the rich benefits a more frugal and self-sustaining style of management allows.

Despite these recent lapses, environmental leadership is now emerging that will capitalize on the many noneconomic strengths America has: a remarkably informed citizenry and a top-notch scientific and engineering community. The certainty of national security, the many legal guarantees, and the many intangible business benefits of working in a secure society will still attract the most useful inventors to America throughout the twenty-first century. The task before us is how to focus that talent on industry's many environmental and energy needs.

Government must play the role of gatekeeper of innovation, joining industry and the research community to foster creative solutions to energy and environmental problems. This is not a Democratic or Republican issue: it is a national issue vital to our future.

America's senior managers, as well as those of other nations, are now waking up to the new environmental agenda governing modern markets. This agenda is exemplified by the principles announced at the 1989 Green Summit in Paris, which included an implicit call for the global economy to phase out the fossil fuels that power the petrochemical treadmill, a treadmill whose hypnotic and perverse pace has enslaved most nations for far too long.

Renewed focus on the environment by the world's seven top industrialized nations has prompted *The Economist* to make this astute observation: "What defense has been to the world's leaders for the past 40 years, the environment will be for the next 40: an attractive exercise in national self-restraint, where gains depend less on what individual countries do than on whether many countries trust each other."

After all, national security concerns are now intimately connected to environmental issues. Consider the following observation by Michael G. Renner, a senior researcher at the Worldwatch Institute who specializes in disarmament:

> Interdependence in the military, economic and ecological realms is now a fact of life. It has already begun to erode traditional notions of security and even national sovereignty itself. "Security" is commonly associated with safety against foreign attack. But in an age of unparalleled environmental destruction, a reasonable definition of security needs to encompass breathable air and potable water, safety from toxic and radioactive hazards, and protection from the loss of topsoil that assures us our daily bread.

The remarkable good news is that more and more Americans are sharing this thought. From ordinary citizen to expert, from the old guard to the new, a great shift in emphasis is occurring that may mean as much to American revitalization throughout the 1990s as the destruction of the Berlin Wall has meant for Europe in 1989–90.

What we have been doing so well for so long in the fields of defense and medicine, we now need to do in energy products and environmental technology—namely, market innovations and sell efficiency. We must become free to make money on environmental upgrades, not remain captives of a mindset preoccupied with a limited sense of government, regulation, and opportunity.

Today's environmental issues—from acid rain and urban smog to the Great Lakes' toxins and the weapons-complex cleanup—will not easily be answered by sterile, bureaucratic platforms. These problems demand social input; only when the technical community joins with the citizenry can excellence be achieved. After all, it is human beings who create pollution and it is human beings who will clean it up. The human race, as Robert Ornstein and Paul Ehrlich note in *New World, New Mind,* needs to replace the "just one more beer can thrown out the window" mindset with a new way of thinking, one that responds adequately to the patterns of environmental abuse.

The earth has definite limits, an assimilative capacity which we can't safely go beyond without severe consequences. The Greeks and Romans, and now we Americans, have tested these boundaries. Our Great Plains and Great Lakes, along with the sooty signature of today's Grand Canyon, are but a few examples among many. As icons of our contemporary problems, they serve to epitomize billions of offenses this grand old earth has weathered.

Our point here is simple: History is a warning. As we enter the 1990s, a time when international competition and national security are intimately linked with improvements in environmental management, we must remember that government *and* citizens have a shared role. Instead of getting government off our backs, we need it to pick us up off the ground.

Chapter 2

Nuclear Weapons: The Cost and the Cleanup

If there ever was an element that deserved a name associated with hell, it is plutonium. This is not only because of its use in atomic bombs—which certainly would amply qualify it—but also because of its fiendishly toxic properties, even in small amounts.

—Robert E. Wilson

Plutonium is so toxic that if inhaled, a speck the size of a dust particle can cause lung cancer. Because of its intense flammability, plutonium is stockpiled in small, isolated quantities, which explains why many hundreds of small pockets of it are found across the vast U.S. nuclear-weapons complex. Robert Wilson's comment is significant, since he was a key manager of the nuclear power industry when it was still in its infancy. Much that has happened since bears a direct warning about the industrialized world's romance with the atom.

The most significant recent news about our use of the atom comes from the federal General Accounting Office (GAO), an independent budget review agency. GAO now reports that cleaning up the wastes of our nuclear-arms production facilities will cost between $130 and $300 billion. To put that figure in perspective, consider that the federal government spent $160 billion on all domestic discretionary programs last year. That's everything from law enforcement to science programs to health research.

Naomi Shohno, a nuclear physicist and author of *The Legacy of Hiroshima*, calculated the amount of radioactivity stemming from this massive amount of weapons production: "It is as if 91 rounds of Hiroshima-size atomic bombs had been produced each day of the 40 years that have passed since the end of World War II."[1]

Most of this radioactivity remains at the weapons production sites. Senator John Glenn of Ohio, chairman of the Senate Committee on Governmental Affairs, noted in 1989 that the problems found at Love Canal "are like a drop in the Pacific Ocean" when compared to the weapon sites scattered across the country. Glenn estimated that, over the next twenty years, it will cost $244 billion to fund continued nuclear-weapons production, existing related environment, health, and safety programs, and the cleanup of past mistakes.

"There is no question about the seriousness of the cleanup," confirmed Robert K. Dawson, President Ronald Reagan's top budget manager for natural resources, energy, and science programs. The effort will "require a significant dedication of federal funds," he added. But the real choice before the president is "How safe is safe?" continued Dawson; decisions to expend limited federal monies will hinge on a series of tough political choices. Among them is whether to start rehabilitating a large number of sites, or to concentrate financial resources on a few high-visibility "deluxe model" hot spots, such as the Hanford Reservation in the state of Washington.

There are probably over eight hundred contaminated sites associated with nuclear-bomb production throughout the United States.[2] Upgrading production capacity at these various pieces of the intricate production puzzle will cost tens of billions of dollars. In addition, insiders at the President's Office of Management and Budget, the National Security Council, and the Environmental Protection Agency now suggest that the environmental restoration of these same facilities will cost perhaps twice as much as the upgrade itself. Add to these astounding amounts the costs of long-term storage of ever-accumulating radioactive waste, and the cost will reach hundreds of billions.[3]

Why must taxpayers now face such enormous cleanup bills? In exchange for building a needed national defense system, the military industrial complex won exemptions from many of the laws that govern corporate America, including the Clean Water, Clean

Air and the National Environmental Policy Acts. One of the several ways that arms-production facilities have skirted regulations has been to mix hazardous and radioactive wastes, thereby circumventing laws that pertain to either substance. Until quite recently, this mixed-waste subterfuge allowed tons of radioactive toxics to be dumped into the ground like common garbage.[4]

Right now, no one knows where all the money is going to come from to pay the cleanup bill, a bill that will exceed by far the cost of John F. Kennedy's pursuit of the moon. George Bush, and each of his successors into the next century, will face that unpleasant mission. It will be the largest public-works project in world history.

Hanford: The Beginning of the End

After World War II, low-level radioactive wastes were dumped directly into the ground throughout the United States because it was thought the soil would dilute these dangerous materials to harmless levels. When dried, these wastes were, on occasion, stuffed into cardboard boxes and rototilled into the soil. At DOE's Hanford weapon-production site in the state of Washington, some 200 billion gallons of radioactive waste were also dumped into various ponds and pits, or pumped directly into groundwater. According to recently released contractor documents, the Columbia River, a major nesting area for our national symbol, the bald eagle, and the lifeblood of the Pacific Northwest, was used as a wash sink for Hanford's first operating reactors.

The Hanford Reservation comprises 365,000 acres, or 570 square miles. It takes several hours to circle the reservation by car traveling at a very brisk clip. Just north of where the Yakima and Snake rivers join with the Columbia, this site was selected early in 1943 as the place to build America's first full-size reactors to produce enough plutonium for nuclear warheads, including the bomb that destroyed Nagasaki.

Hanford is where America's full-scale experiment with massive arms production began. At present, at least eighty-one separate areas on the reservation have sufficiently severe toxic contamination to qualify for the Superfund National Priorities List, a roster of the nation's most contaminated sites. Hanford is budgeted to absorb $46 billion in tax dollars for cleanup and restoration.[5]

THE WEAPONS COMPLEX

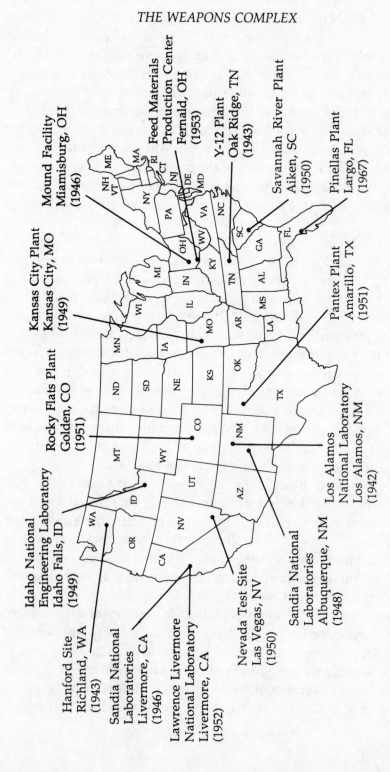

Feed Materials
Production Center
Fernald, OH
(1953)

Y-12 Plant
Oak Ridge, TN
(1943)

Savannah River Plant
Aiken, SC
(1950)

Mound Facility
Miamisburg, OH
(1946)

Pinellas Plant
Largo, FL
(1967)

Kansas City Plant
Kansas City, MO
(1949)

Pantex Plant
Amarillo, TX
(1951)

Rocky Flats Plant
Golden, CO
(1951)

Los Alamos
National Laboratory
Los Alamos, NM
(1942)

Idaho National
Engineering Laboratory
Idaho Falls, ID
(1949)

Sandia National
Laboratories
Albuquerque, NM
(1948)

Hanford Site
Richland, WA
(1943)

Sandia National
Laboratories
Livermore, CA
(1946)

Lawrence Livermore
National Laboratory
Livermore, CA
(1952)

Nevada Test Site
Las Vegas, NV
(1950)

Source: U.S. Department of Energy (U.S. Government Printing Office)

ENVIRONMENTAL RESTORATION MONIES FOR THE HANFORD
SITE (IN MILLIONS OF DOLLARS)

	Fiscal Year							
	1988	*1989*	*1990*	*1991*	*1992*	*1993*	*1994*	*1995*
Environment								
Base Program	61.0	58.5	73.6	88.2	103.9	96.0	92.0	95.0
Corrective Actions								
Air	3.6	0.9	0.7	0.7	0.7	0.7	0.7	0.7
Water	2.9	2.7	1.2	1.2	0.7	1.4	1.3	1.3
Solid Waste Management	34.5	51.7	70.1	108.4	119.1	98.8	87.6	69.7
Remedial Action	15.5	17.8	19.8	60.8	90.5	150.5	150.8	150.8
Subtotal	117.5	131.6	165.4	259.3	314.9	347.4	332.4	317.5
Safety and Health								
Base Program	39.1	31.3	40.7	63.4	50.7	31.4	26.0	25.7
Corrective Actions								
Nuclear Reactor	33.1	22.0	10.5	5.7	3.6	3.5	2.6	2.6
Nonreactor Nuclear	5.7	6.4	6.4	8.2	13.8	5.3	5.4	5.4
Subtotal	77.9	59.7	57.6	77.3	68.1	40.2	34.0	33.7
Total	195.4	191.3	223.0	336.6	383.0	387.6	366.4	351.2

Source: U.S. Dept. of Energy

Today, Hanford is undergoing a transformation to become the first in a long list of nuclear national sacrifice zones, areas of the country abandoned because of the unaffordable costs of bringing them back to useful, safe life. Though many other parts of the country are currently facing a similar prognosis, Hanford's tale leaves behind some sizable footprints.[6]

Though much of the world has been appalled by reports of the Soviet Union's experience with nuclear-weapons testing and reactors such as Chernobyl, few realize that the United States has also inherited its share of nuclear tragedies. Recently, Soviet officials have been forced to embrace such drastic measures as installing radiation detectors in homes because of disease and illnesses attributed to widespread nuclear contamination. Although still exempt from such ubiquitous off-site contamination, America is just beginning to discover the tragic legacy of post–World War II weapons production.

The secrecy of Soviet society has, until the last few years, been central to its sense of self.[7] A Soviet lecturer made these observations in May 1989: "Unmarked burial sites containing radioactive waste from production, science and medicine—various ampules, flasks, gowns and a host of other 'contaminated' items—lie near virtually every major industrial center. People do not know about them. They cut grass nearby, graze livestock, go out and enjoy nature." America, despite its authentic commitment to open government, also surrounded its weapons complex with a shroud of technical elitism. Senior management deliberately avoided logical environmental controls and fostered a cult of environmental irresponsibility.

Hanford is a radioactive graveyard, home to approximately half (123 out of 226) of the nation's inactive reactors, reprocessing plants, and vaults, which have threatened worker safety and taxed the environment since the 1940s. These eerie structures will serve as "lasting monuments to our romance with the atom," observes Robert Alvarez, an Environmental Policy Institute specialist now working for the Senate Government Affairs Committee.

The abandonment of Hanford is going to have a devastating impact on the local economy because, notes Alvarez, "plutonium and wheat don't mix." Wheat farmers dominate this dry, desert-like eastern portion of Washington State. Alvarez speculated that the long-lived radioactive threat to cities such as Richland and Pasco will drive investors and jobs away, leaving behind ghost towns.

The warning signs are already there. Some Mormons, who for generations have worked the crop fields downwind of Hanford, now often refuse to eat the fruits of their own labor. Instead, they send their produce to markets in Seattle and Portland, where unsuspecting Americans continue to provide a market for the unwanted food.[8]

The health threats to lifelong Hanford employees and people living in the vicinity are also alarming. Back in 1948, a shiny new stack at the facility leaked. The chief on-site physicist told the advisory committee on biology and medicine in October 1948 that workers were being exposed to 10-rem-per-day plutonium lung doses. (One rem is a dose of ionizing radiation that produces a biological effect equal to that of the average X-ray exam.) The committee maintained that this safety threat was no reason to stop production. Exposing American workers to 10 X-rays per day is illegal today, a deliberate crime punishable by the courts.

At the time of these exposures, Hanford was the "world's largest trailer park"; some forty thousand to fifty thousand people lived on site. Many of them, including children, were exposed to dangerous doses of radiation. But Hanford has never hidden its affiliation with the arms race. The team logo of Hanford High School is a mushroom cloud. Residents living near Hanford do not hide throat-tumor scars allegedly caused by widespread radioactive contamination.

Hanford's designation as the nation's first sacrifice zone is appropriate. This is where our commitment to plutonium production began. This is also where it will, in a palpable sense, end. No matter how severe the regional economic consequences, we will never be able to restore this part of the country to its former magnificence.

Perhaps we shouldn't try. "I learned when I ran the Army Corps of Engineers that whenever you locate large energy projects, or massive water efforts, or now this billion-dollar nuclear-waste cleanup project, that you can't make decisions on regional economic impacts," observes Robert Dawson. In spite of this rule, even Dawson admits that the size of the mistake at Hanford "is so large, there probably ought to be some social programs to ease the pain."

The U.S. government decided in 1988 to place Hanford "in cold standby," meaning that the facility has become a remediation project rather than a production unit supplying military needs. This gesture marks the beginning of major changes in the way America defends itself and the environment. It also represents a major political concession by the federal government, which is now telling thousands of Americans that the jobs they've held most of their lives will someday be gone. In addition, government-based miscalculations made in haste by national security experts may have, in the aggregate, sacrificed these Americans' health and their neighborhoods.

Future generations may come to realize that the chain-link fence now separating them from the Hanford reservation represents the technological and political equivalent of our retreat from Vietnam. In Vietnam, our night vision, silent planes, and high-powered equipment proved ineffective in the Southeast Asian jungles; at

Hanford, our arms-production policymakers ignored the limits of primitive waste-treatment technologies. Our pullout at Hanford, like our pullout in Vietnam, is a major political concession. It speaks to the American people's desire to move beyond a blind trust in nature.

Savannah: A Separate Culture

One might ask how such a legacy of errors could accumulate.

To understand the answer to this question, we must recognize that these facilities operated in a separate, secret culture that froze out the realities of new emerging technologies and environmental concerns. Keith Fultz of the GAO has noted that "It is the biggest failure of our federal government." A series of inquiries by Fultz have revealed that the most dangerous industrial processes known to man have been carried out by operators often paid less than custodial workers and with a frantic emphasis on production over health and safety issues.

In July 1988, inspectors at the Savannah River Plant (SRP) in

RESTORING SAVANNAH RIVER (IN MILLIONS OF DOLLARS)

	1988	1989	1990	1991	1992	1993	1994	1995
				Fiscal Year				
Environment								
Base Program	62	67	67	75	68	70	73	75
Corrective Actions								
Air	2	0	8	13	10	16	6	8
Water	11	8	25	48	35	15	10	10
Solid Waste Management	29	41	49	27	52	54	45	79
Remedial Action	18	44	70	50	66	43	12	29
Subtotal	122	160	219	213	231	198	146	201
Safety and Health								
Base Program	106	118	130	135	135	135	135	135
Corrective Actions								
Nuclear Reactor	34	52	62	84	100	100	100	100
Nonreactor Nuclear	4	4	5	28	55	55	55	55
Nonnuclear	10	9	9	42	45	45	45	45
Subtotal	154	183	206	289	335	335	335	335
Total	276	343	425	502	566	533	481	536

Source: U.S. Dept. of Energy

Aiken, South Carolina, were shocked to find that operating crews knew none of the standard safety procedures, such as ultrasonic testing for cracks in reactors. These procedures have been mandated at all U.S. commercial nuclear reactors since the 1979 accident at Three Mile Island. The DOE has promised that they would test the Savannah reactors amid consistent requests for more detailed looks at cracks, but tests have been stalled because of fears that the public won't allow production to continue. "The DOE can't afford to let Congress know how bad it is, and we as a nation can't afford to clean it up," suggests Fultz.

Stretching over 192,323 acres, the SRP is the most radioactive site in the world. A three-hundred-square-mile domain spread across three different counties in South Carolina, it is only twelve miles south of Aiken, and employed a staff of between twelve thousand and sixteen thousand in recent years.

Historically, SRP produced the major portion of plutonium and all tritium—a radioactive gas that decays slowly and is considered a key strategic concern—required for weapons. Also the sole producer of heavy water in the U.S. until 1982, SRP now is the only producer in the U.S. of tritium, plutonium 238, and heavy water. Over three-fourths of America's high-level nuclear wastes—over 1 billion curies in concentration—currently sit near the Savannah reactors. These wastes contain fission products, traces of uranium and plutonium, as well as "hot spots" of transuranic elements. These latter are the leftovers from chemical processing.

Many experts worry that Savannah is an inadequate site to store such wastes. The site sits on top of a major freshwater aquifer that supplies drinking water for several southeastern states. This area has high rainfall, which speeds up the movement of toxins into groundwater, and sits in the middle of an area that experienced the 1886 Charleston quake. The worst recorded earthquake on the eastern seaboard, it has been described as the San Francisco quake of the South.

The most recent warning sign at Savannah occurred in August 1988, when a Chernobyl-type disaster was barely averted by the operators of the facility—the Du Pont Corporation. Operators were starting up the reactor, a procedure which primarily consists of lifting control rods. These control rods capture neutrons when they are in the reactor. When they are lifted up, the neutrons pass to other control rods, fission increases, and a chain reaction develops resulting in the production of nuclear power. The operators continued to pull the rods higher and higher, and yet the reactor would not start. It was finally shut down after the rods had been lifted far beyond their limits.

According to John Ahearne, a man who comes from the civilian commercial nuclear power industry and now heads the weapons complex's Nuclear Safety Board for President Bush, there is a grave danger in forging ahead under these circumstances. It is akin, he claims, to flooring your accelerator when at a stoplight with your left foot on the brake. Eventually, violently, you jolt forward. With a reactor, such a buildup of enormous energy can be lethal, as two operators discovered at an experimental breeder reactor in Idaho several years back. One yanked up a rod to see what the holdup was, and both were impaled on the ceiling.

"The most disturbing thing about the operators at Savannah is that they didn't know what they were doing. You shouldn't run reactors until the operators know what they are doing," notes Ahearne. (Savannah's reactors have been shut down at four times the average rate for civilian reactors.)

The Savannah operators' ineptitude came to light during that same summer of 1988, when a team of DOE inspectors discovered flush pipes beneath Savannah's P-reactor. Flush pipes were part of a 1950s system designed to rapidly cool down a reactor in the event of a malfunction or meltdown. Since this system relied upon a direct discharge of radioactivity into the environment, flush pipes were long ago eliminated from operations of reactors throughout the world.

The seventy inspectors were engaged in a "walk-down"—a design inventory term used by safety experts—at the P-reactor, when they found the two flush pipes that Savannah operators had forgotten about for three decades. While apparently they were never used, the possibility that the flush pipes might have been deployed was disturbing enough. "Even Du Pont got religion when they found this out," commented one of the DOE inspectors. (Du Pont operated Savannah from its initiation.)

DOE's Richard Starostecki claimed that "with such deliberate lack of self-questioning and external review, it was impossible to make rational decisions. Du Pont's environmental, safety, and health [commonly referred to as ES&H] programs were nothing more than malicious compliance." He explained this description by noting that Du Pont repeatedly told DOE to "Trust us, we do a good job." Instead of establishing an integrated ES&H oversight program, however, Du Pont created a puppet assurance program and "coordination for the various components was always someone else's job—and that someone didn't exist."

According to Starostecki, the facilities at the Savannah River Plant were state-of-the-art in the early 1950s. By the seventies, however, the operators there had become "a closed community and never interacted with peers. They put up a big fence intellectually." And when questioned about safety concerns, "they put up an even higher fence." Starostecki claimed that Du Pont was aware of the magnitude of the problem some fourteen years ago. An internal study by Du Pont admits that careless dumping over the course of previous decades had already resulted in contamination that will exist "for centuries or millennia."

Du Pont built and has operated Savannah since 1951. On April 1, 1989, however, it passed the baton to Westinghouse. As reported by *The New York Times,* incoming Westinghouse managers of the Savannah production complex now estimate that the costs of maintaining the production of tritium will be four times previous estimates. This rising price tag more accurately reflects the real costs borne by the separate culture that held sway at Savannah. It also underscores the price to be paid for safer environmental management.

The arrival of Westinghouse signals the start of a new era at Savannah. The firm has also taken over at Hanford and Fernald, Ohio—another old weapons-complex facility—and is hoping to utilize its vast arsenal of underexercised nuclear expertise. Since Westinghouse constructed roughly half of the world's commercial reactors, it has positioned itself to rechannel that expertise. In addition, since the government absolves contractors from all liabilities caused by nuclear negligence, Westinghouse is assured of turning a tidy profit.[9] Estimates say that beginning in 1990, between $45 and $50 million a year in profits will accrue to the firm from nuclear-weapons production work, about a fifth of that coming from Savannah.

"It is sort of a no-lose situation from a financial viewpoint," concedes Theodore Stern, executive vice president. "Our participation will keep Westinghouse in the forefront of nuclear technology and help maintain its leadership in commercial nuclear power," adds Chris Newton, a Westinghouse spokesman. "DOE contracts keep Westinghouse nuclear managers, scientists, and engineers active and productive," he added. Westinghouse has not received a new nuclear construction contract in about a decade.[10]

No matter what its motivations, Westinghouse promises to be more open and progressive in its policies and technology. Because signs of cracking appear on three Savannah reactors that are well over thirty years of age, safety upgrades will now be installed to detect cooling pipe leaks. At present, the company is also busy developing new technologies that would glassify and solidify the most dangerous Savannah River Plant wastes. Once this project is fully operational in 1992, it will take twelve years to convert the 33 million gallons of radioactive waste that have accumulated at Savannah since 1954.

Accountability: Fernald and Rocky Flats

Apportioning blame for the damage rendered by our nation's weapons complex is a difficult task. Quantifying the costs of the environmental damage at both Hanford and Savannah is beyond the realm of simple mathematics and technical expertise. An even more challenging (and gruesome) chore is reimbursing families who feel they have been harmed.

The Feeds Materials Production Center in Fernald, Ohio, is the third-largest radioactive waste dump in the United States. Twenty miles northwest of Cincinnati, the FMPC is a 1,050-acre site, less than $\frac{1}{300}$ the size of Hanford. Yet it hosts an extensive arsenal of facilities that can process and reprocess uranium. In concrete silos it houses uranium residues from the Manhattan Project of the 1940s—America's first bomb-building effort. Over a million people, primarily in nearby Cincinnati, live within a twenty-mile radius of this plant. According to one estimate, since 1945 some 385,000 pounds of uranium dust have been released into the atmosphere from Fernald. Thirty times this amount—12 million pounds—has been dumped in waste pits now seeping into some water supplies.

Because uranium dust is heavy, it is assumed that most of the airborne radioactivity settled near the site. One study postulates that children living nearby could have received up to 400 rems in radioactivity from accidental airborne releases. Such accidents, experts estimate, account for twenty-two percent of the uranium contamination in the area.[11]

The details of mismanagement at Fernald are shocking, but consistent. In testimony before senate investigators, Fernald plant worker Jesse Abney revealed that he had been assured that contamination at the work site was at an "acceptable" level. Moreover, he was never told what radioactive substances to avoid on the site. In April 1987, he discovered he was contaminated with plutonium. "We are tired of being patted on the back and sent our way. We are tired of platitudes. We are tired of being ignored by our government," he stated during an emotional set of briefings before Congress in 1989.

In 1984, a baghouse designed to prevent uranium dust from escaping into the air at Fernald malfunctioned, setting off an alarm. The response was not to fix the baghouse, but to recalibrate the alarm so that it would no longer warn when releases occurred.

Some contractors apparently petitioned for safety improvements, but were turned down. In 1980, NLO, Inc., the contractor running the facility at Fernald, requested funds from the DOE to build a basin to capture storm-water runoff from the site. Though the contract with DOE stated that it was the DOE's responsibility to supply such simple yet crucial safety upgrades, the DOE maintained that funds were not available.[12]

When the basin was constructed it violated Environmental Protection Agency standards: because of an engineering design mishap, it was made too small. Plans for a biodenitrification facility to treat the enormous amounts of nitrates that have been polluting the Great Miami River and local groundwater were also put off, allegedly because of budget concerns. Though construction of this latter treatment system has now begun, it is still not up to standards three years after deadline. By shortchanging these basic construction needs, DOE was able to spend the savings on bomb production instead. The result: the much larger cleanup tab we are now facing.

This pattern of funding bomb production at the cost of safety extends to the Rocky Mountains' urban jewel—Denver, Colorado. Who would think that the country's most dangerous radioactive hot spot would lie in one of the world's most spectacular mountain ranges? Hillside 881, which has relatively low levels of strontium and cesium (two products of nuclear fission) is rated as the highest danger by the EPA because of its proximity to public drinking-water reservoirs. (Hanford and Savannah are hotter, but they are also farther from human populations.)

Rocky Flats, just sixteen miles northwest of Denver, also illustrates our tale of blind trust in nature. The worst accident in the history of the U.S. weapons complex occurred here in May 1969 when plutonium ignited, starting a $50 million blaze. After the fire, readings revealed radioactivity more than 200 times higher than the normal background level. A previous fire—in September 1957—had resulted in the dispersal of fine plutonium and uranium dust throughout Jefferson County. The late Carl J. Johnson, a former local health officer who helped victims recover settlements, discovered that between 1947 and 1952, the death rate for Jefferson County was below the national average. Between 1957 and 1962, however, the local death rate rose to twice the national average. A study conducted by Johnson in 1980 also revealed that Rocky Flats workers had eight times as many brain tumors as would be expected from the sample population.[13]

Both fires at Rocky Flats raged out of control because simple safety upgrades, such as the use of nonflammable glovebox materials, had not been made due to budget constraints. In addition, drums stored on site leaked oil contaminated with plutonium. As a result, the federal government has purchased huge tracts of land east and southeast of Rocky Flats, sealing off yet another sacrifice zone from the public. Unfortunately, this area is now teeming with wildlife. The impact that this tainted environment will have on the future generations of birds, deer, and other animals now residing within this fortress remains unstudied.

More recently, the Federal Bureau of Investigation has reported that clandestine dumping and burning of radioactive wastes oc-

COLLECTIVE RADIATION DOSE TO WORKERS 1980–1988

Year	Number of Plants	Annual Collective Dose (person-rems)	Average Collective Dose Per Reactor (person-rems)
1980	68	53,796	791
1981	70	54,142	773
1982	74	52,190	705
1983	75	56,471	753
1984	78	55,214	708
1985	82	43,042	525
1986	88	42,664	485
1987	97	40,702	420
1988	102	40,841	400

Source: U.S. Nuclear Regulatory Commission

WORKERS EXPOSED TO RADIATION 1980–1988

Year	Number of Plants	Total Number Exposed	Average Per Reactor
1980	68	80,331	1181
1981	70	82,183	1174
1982	74	84,382	1140
1983	75	85,646	1142
1984*	78	98,092	1258
1985†	82	92,871	1132
1986	88	100,924	1147
1987	97	104,458	1077
1988	102	103,227	1012
Total 1980–1988		832,114 workers exposed	

* In 1984 Humboldt Bay and Indian Point 1 were closed and are no longer included in this count of reactors.

† In 1985 it was decided that Dresden 1, a plant that had been shut down since October 1978, would not be put into commercial operation again and it is not included in this count of reactors.

Source: U.S. Nuclear Regulatory Commission

curred at Rocky Flats during December of 1988. The bitter irony
of this and other discoveries is that the operator of Rocky Flats—
Rockwell International—was awarded $8.6 million in bonuses
from the DOE in May 1987 for "excellent" management. This
despite departmental acknowledgments that waste-treatment facilities there were "patently illegal" and had resulted in "serious
contamination."[14]

Epidemiological studies are now being conducted at most
weapons-production sites to confirm the range of suspected cancers and other diseases. But even if the results prove conclusive,
local residents at Fernald and Rocky Flats shouldn't expect much
compensation soon. The DOE has agreed to pay 24,000 neighbors of the Feeds Materials Production Center $73 million for
emotional distress and the decline of property values, not for
health violations.

It is going to be far more difficult to develop a comprehensive
and equitable compensation policy for the health hazards that
derive from the entire weapons complex. U.S. veterans have won
an important federal compensation package because of their high-
level exposure to radioactivity during weapons-testing duty. They
are a small homogeneous population, so it was possible to design
a formula that would compensate just about any in the group who
could claim a reasonable connection between exposure and health
problems. But the science and the costs are still too mind-boggling
in scale and detail to permit the same to be done for residents near
or in national sacrifice zones. As a result, the people of Hanford,
Savannah, and Fernald will likely wait much longer than the veterans for their compensation.

It took years to get compensatory legislation for the veterans
through all the hoops; it could take decades to pass legislation regarding the weapons sites because of the immense uncertainties in
documenting direct causal health consequences. Weapons production was so secret that the health-test results in this area could prove
meaningless because of incomplete data from the plants themselves. With weapon sites scattered across the country, any kind of
broad-based relief arrangement might also break the federal bank.

The next step, then, should not be a single-minded pursuit of
financial damages from the federal government. Instead, we need

full public input into the cleanup process. What was once unspeakable needs to become part of a public process, a public response. As Sen. John Glenn has observed, one of the biggest lessons learned from this episode in American history is that we should "not just hide everything behind a veil of secrecy like we did for the last 38 years. Now, that doesn't mean that we reveal the amount of weapon material we are producing to the Russians and everybody else to read and know about. What it does mean is that in the future, we cannot ignore the environment, health and safety matters that are rendered necessary to maintain whatever production levels are deemed necessary."

Though the anger that citizens feel toward the perpetrators of these past mistakes is real and legitimate, it is now time to move beyond blame, to begin the process whereby citizens determine the extent to which federal agents must clean up their neighborhoods.

Speaking the Unspeakable: Choosing the Proper Reform Path

Coping with the waste by-products of our weapons complex (as well as those of the commercial nuclear power industry) will force Americans to update their antiquated estimate of nature. The sunshine recently shed on the DOE's arms-production facilities holds promise for a more accurate and humane review of our nation's overall radioactive-waste management plans.

Estimates prepared by the GAO show that well over half of every dollar spent on nuclear production should go toward cleaning up the resulting waste.[15] Despite such recommendations, the White House maintains that adequate funds are available to operate the arms-production plants safely. Overall, the President's Office of Management and Budget (OMB) numbers show a rough 8-to-1 ratio in favor of production over environmental, safety, and health (ES&H) budgets over the course of recent history. OMB has always earmarked more millions each fiscal year for design work on new production reactors than for cleanup on the old ones. This historic inequity can no longer be tolerated as runaway production tactics undermine both national security and public health. How long it will take to achieve the proper ratio between production and safety is still very much an open question.

BEYOND 1995: A SUMMARY OF ENVIRONMENTAL RESTORATION
COSTS (IN MILLIONS OF FY 1990 DOLLARS)

Site	Environment Expected	High	Safety and Health Expected	High
Feed Materials Production Center	$ 963	$ 1,175	$ 84	$ 105
Hanford Site	27,000	46,000	30	130
Idaho National Engineering Laboratory	515	2,050	0	0
Kansas City Plant	5	8	2	3
Lawrence Livermore National Laboratory	60	300	0	0
Los Alamos National Laboratory	907	1,432	110	110
Mount Plant	58	78	0	0
Nevada Test Site	250	750	0	0
Oak Ridge, Y-12 Plant	290	530	50	150
Pantex Plant	104	155	80	80
Pinellas Plant	9	9	0	0
Rocky Flats Plant	120	180	0	0
Sandia National Laboratories/ Albuquerque	55	70	0	0
Sandia National Laboratories/ Livermore	1	3	0	0
Savannah River Plant	349	7,000	800	1,800
Subtotals	$30,686	$59,740	$1,156	$2,388

Total ES&H Expected: $31,842
Total ES&H High: $62,128

Source: U.S. Department of Energy

No matter which is more deserving of the funds—more production or more environmental restoration—the competition for
scarce resources has a long history at the Department of Energy.
"Part of today's problem stems from our attempts to stretch, defer
and absorb budgetary shortfalls, hoping that next year things
would be better, and we could catch up. As a result this country's
ability to produce and maintain a nuclear weapons stockpile is in
serious jeopardy," stated former Energy Secretary John S. Her-

rington in a frank letter to the president shortly before Bush appointed his replacement.

"You know Congress owns a part of the blame [for these past mistakes]," said a Department of Energy manager who prefers to remain anonymous. "It was pork-barrel politics that brought us seventeen thousand jobs at Savannah, and over the years, tens of thousands of jobs at Hanford. Other states also wanted part of the action. That's why we have a Rocky Flats in Colorado or even the national labs such as Sandia in New Mexico and Livermore in California."

Solutions to the dilemma posed by our obsolete arms-production policies go beyond budgets and safety upgrades.[16] The DOE, under the leadership of Secretary James D. Watkins, is also considering a drastic consolidation of its activities. In the twenty-first century, rather than littering the American landscape with many different parts of the production process, the government will build "theme parks" or "super parks" for weapons production.[17]

According to an OMB insider, "Theme parks will allow a smaller production network and the building of smaller and fewer weapons—more bang for the buck."

This evolution in weapons production offers some limited, yet significant, comfort to analysts. "There is every reason to assume these parks will be safer," comments Alvarez, who has followed the issue for over a decade. "If you shrink and consolidate, you cut wastes and cut exposures." He has a new anxiety, however. "What I'm concerned about in this new passion for theme parks is that the one hundred old mistakes will become sacrifice zones."

Yet another critical question arises: Do we really need much more production?

David Albright, of the Union of Concerned Scientists, notes that future arms-reduction efforts and more efficient recycling of warhead materials may be able to at least defer the need for a new tritium production facility. Plutonium, he claims, is in ample supply. Tritium supplies are harder to manage because it decays over time. Since the federal government, for national security reasons, does not disclose current levels of tritium supply, it is hard to say how effectively we can operate with less.

"If there are deep reductions in our nuclear arsenal because of arms treaty negotiations, we would not need to build new production reactors for thirty years," says Albright. He also suggests that the U.S. "minimize our dependence on tritium" and explore nonreactor sources of tritium.

The Los Alamos National Laboratory claims that Soviet production reactors are also old and unsafe and will be shut down soon, a further indication that the world may be reaching a threshold point on weapons production. From both an environmental and an economic perspective, the environmentally sound arms-control policies Albright espouses may deserve greater scrutiny.

Seweryn Bialer and Michael Mandelbaum, authors of the exhaustively researched *Global Rivals,* sum up these production and need questions rather concisely: "The arms race has reached a plateau. The two sides have accumulated enough weapons, and have enough experience in competing with one another to acquire them, to be ready to conclude that neither can achieve a decisive military advantage over the other and that the time has therefore come to settle for a draw."

Having reached this plateau, we now have a panoramic view of the astonishing environmental carnage of the arms race. If we can stop the mad rush to create more and more bombs in a fashion that creates national sacrifice zones within our own borders, then doesn't it also make sense to reevaluate the policies that have absorbed so much talent and research money in the United States for decades?

The process of healing has begun, with Congress playing a leading role by speaking what only yesterday was unspeakable. As one OMB official put it: "We won the war with the bomb. No one wanted to ask questions." Today, hard questions are being asked and cleanup costs are being assessed. Our national security is no longer just the concern of military insiders hell-bent on producing more and more warhead materials. The issue is now being addressed by Congress, government officials, and the general public in order to redirect funds to environmental, safety, and health concerns that have immediate economic and national security consequences.

Our battle against contamination caused by the military complex drills home a most consequential point. For decades, we have been busy building bombs we may never use against an enemy, bombs whose creation, because of shortsighted environmental policies, entails the slow death of our own citizens and wildlife. The stately bald eagle now finds that one of its homes, the Columbia River near Hanford, is littered with radioactive debris inherited from the decisions of security-minded policymakers who, ironically, invoked its image as a sign of American pride and strength. Its soaring silhouette now represents a new kind of sacrifice.

One needs only to look to the Soviet Union to see the crippling effect a secretive and all-consuming race to produce nuclear weapons can have on an economy and a people if the plans of military advocates are placed, without question, above the long-term resource needs of the nation. Another comment from *Global Rivals* illustrates this point: "The accumulation of more and more armaments not only was not necessarily an asset for the Soviet Union, it turned out to be a liability. It acted as a draw on the economy, with a substantial fraction of the gross domestic output—perhaps as much as 20 percent—going to military uses. And with the best scientists, technicians and machines assigned to the military sector, the civilian economy suffered."

Twenty percent of gross output translates into the equivalent of one business day per week lost for an entire nation. Some say this is the fundamental fact behind Gorbachev's venture into less centralized Soviet planning.

Some of these observations also ring true for America. The long-term health of the U.S. economy will suffer as a result of the hundreds of billions of dollars' worth of environmental damage experienced at weapons-production sites. Perhaps the primary difference between the two nations' dilemmas is the scope of the sacrifice zones. While Hanford measures 570 square miles, the Ural national sacrifice zone is about eighty times that size.

Now that a new openness is allowing us to reassess the need for an arms race, perhaps the better way to build national security is to develop a robust economy guided by environmental excellence. A single-minded preoccupation with defense has begun to stunt this country's economic muscle as Japan and the less defense-oriented nations gain on us. It is time to go back on the offensive with a new set of more affordable beliefs.

There never has been environmental protection in America. There has been remediation, the expensive correcting and lessening of mistakes; but not full-scale prevention. Today, more than ever, White House and corporate decision-makers must begin this bolder, more restrained path of self-protection.

Finding a New Affordability

America's experience with the nuclear-weapons complex should weigh heavily on the conscience of those who now push the commercial nuclear power industry as an answer to the problem of global warming. Representatives from the commercial nuclear power industry are right to point out how DOE facilities flunked many of their standard NRC procedures and precautions; but many of the environmental hazards of the weapons plants also occur in the commercial sphere, even at the best-handled sites.[18]

The link between nuclear-weapons production and commercial nuclear power is radioactive waste, mountains of it, buried underground.

Again, the GAO paints an unsettling but honest picture. Decommissioning the first one hundred nuclear power plants operating in this country could result in another series of less severe, yet significant, national sacrifice zones. According to a report issued in August of 1989, groundwater levels at five of eight nuclear-fuel processing facilities studied exceeded government standards by 730 times. Soil contamination was as high as 320 times the standard at three of the studied facilities. The purpose of this GAO study was to show the potential magnitude of contamination from commercial facilities as they reach their retiring age and begin to be dismantled in the 1990s.[19]

Keith Fultz warned that the decommissioning of California's Rancho Seco, the nation's first large nuclear power plant to undergo the shutdown process, would reveal even more severe levels of radioactivity than is presently admitted to by the nuclear-industry establishment. GAO found that the substances stored at commercial reactors are "high-level nuclear waste, and the contamination exists within the reactor."

According to Fultz, the NRC "lacks the regulatory teeth" to require an adequate cleanup after an operating license is terminated. He pointed out that the federal government has had to foot a cleanup bill of approximately $400,000 along the Appalachian National Scenic Trail in New York because the NRC did not have the authority to go after the original licensee.

"We, as a nation, are just in what I would call the infancy stage of decommissioning and decontaminating the nuclear facilities that we have," observed Fultz. "There are many similarities between the commercial nuclear industry and what we've just said about the weapons complex: inadequate recordkeeping, buried waste leaking into groundwater supplies, a separate culture not yet up to speed with the American public's lack of confidence in the nuclear establishment." Fultz sums up the uneasiness: "I think the waste problem is the Achilles' heel of the nuclear power industry. Unless we close the loop and solve the problem of nuclear waste, the entire nuclear power industry is in jeopardy."[20]

Ratepayers of the Sacramento Municipal Utility District

U.S. NUCLEAR REACTORS 1980–1989

Year	Number of Reactors Canceled	Reactors Deferred or Delayed	Number of Reactors Completed
1980	16	0	2
1981	6	0	4
1982	18	0	4
1983	6	0	3
1984	6	2	6
1985	2	2	8
1986	2	0	6
1987	0	0	8
1988	3	2	3
1989	1	0	2
TOTAL	60	6	46

NOTE: this list does not include the Seabrook 1 and Shoreham reactors which have been completed but are not yet operating.

Sources: U.S. Department of Energy, *Cleveland Plain Dealer*, Tennessee Valley Authority, *The Wall Street Journal*, Washington Public Power Supply System.

(SMUD) voted to close Rancho Seco, the only nuclear power plant owned by a municipal utility district, in June 1989. Described by Ralph Nader's Public Citizen as a true "lemon," Rancho Seco has a long and telling history. In fact, unknown to dignitaries and spectators, the reactor underwent an emergency shutdown during its grand opening celebrations.

The fifteen-year-old reactor had a lifetime operating average of less than forty percent. It absorbed $400 million in repairs during a two-and-a-half-year outage, beginning in December 1985. After restart in the spring of 1988, the plant continued to perform erratically, suffering another shutdown in 1989, on the anniversary of the Three Mile Island accident. The two contractors who built and designed the reactor—Bechtel Corporation and Babcock & Wilcox—offered the board a last-minute unprecedented risk-sharing operation contract just before a June 1989 vote on the fate of the plant. But voters, focusing on the economics of the plant, were not convinced.[21]

Interestingly, the SMUD board then interpreted the vote to mean only that SMUD could no longer operate the plant, but that someone else could. In stepped the Quadrex Corp., an upstart firm hailing from the Silicon Valley, which announced a bold venture to have SMUD transfer operations to a consortium of private interests who would take on all the nuclear liabilities and sell power to turn a profit.

This venture too failed after extended negotiations. Though Wall Street investors were willing to bet on Quadrex chief executive officer William Derrickson (once described as "a manager with chutzpah"), who had helped turn around nuclear management nightmares elsewhere, the numbers just no longer added up favorably.

While the effort to close Rancho Seco required several public votes, on the other side of the country another nuclear power debate highlighted how a new generation of strong-willed politicians now want to lead the nation out of its nuclear nightmares. This time, instead of national corporate interests trying to override local sentiments, it was the federal government trying to pull rank on state and local officials.

In a bold move, the Shoreham reactor would be sold by its

owner, Long Island Power and Light Co., to the Long Island Power Authority (LIPA) for the grand sum of $1. (Ironically, at one point, it was proposed that Rancho Seco be sold for the same simple sum.) LIPA would then contract with the New York Power Authority to decommission the mess.

All along, the principal concern of local officials was that the $5.5 billion Shoreham nuclear plant, originally budgeted at $70 million, might be unsafe. Construction of the 809-megawatt reactor, located fifty-five miles east of Manhattan, was completed in 1983. NRC regulations, however, required that the local government prepare an emergency evacuation plan for use in the event of an accident. The dreadful thought of an emergency evacuation on Long Island, with its well-known traffic congestion, was enough to convince many local officials that the plant was not viable. Whereas many arguments against Rancho Seco hinged on financial analyses that showed how rates might climb with continued reliance on the erratic reactor, Long Island ratepayers face huge increases in their bills *without* Shoreham, a reactor which has not produced one kilowatt of power for public use.

The test of political wills between New York Governor Mario Cuomo and President George Bush,[22] exemplified by a series of legal briefs and personal attacks, played out a contemporary drama—twenty years in the making—that will echo repeatedly throughout the nation during the nineties. Battling against the federal government's massive investment and sizable subsidy of nuclear power, Cuomo is demonstrating the type of courage more and more state leaders are mustering.

Chernobyl cannot be ignored by American planners either, for it epitomizes how a severe nuclear accident carries so many international health consequences. The steep economic toll of Chernobyl is being heard throughout the world. Contaminated food such as beef, cheese, and even chocolate—from nations as far away from the reactor as Britain, Italy, and Holland—were rejected by importers due to fears or evidence of radioactive contamination.

The domestic nuclear industry is correct when they chant about how a direct replica of Chernobyl will never occur in the States. Nonetheless, Sweden, a country that uses more nuclear power per

TOTAL AMERICAN DEFENSE COMPLEX FUNDING (BILLIONS OF
DOLLARS) 1990–2010

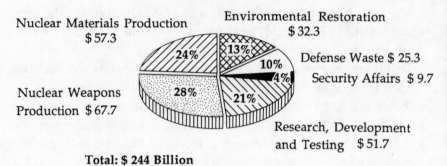

Nuclear Materials Production
$ 57.3

Environmental Restoration
$ 32.3

Defense Waste $ 25.3

Security Affairs $ 9.7

Nuclear Weapons
Production $ 67.7

Research, Development
and Testing $ 51.7

Total: $ 244 Billion

Source: "Report from the President: Modernization Study," U. S. Government Printing
Office, March 1989.

capita than any other nation and has the world's lowest reactor
operating costs,[23] will completely phase out nuclear power by the
next century because of the accident. Witnessing firsthand the
destruction caused by Chernobyl—which almost destroyed the
livelihood of the ten thousand nomadic Lapps living off the rein-
deer and fish in northern Sweden—the progressive Swedish government took the kind of bold steps that today's environment
demands of policymakers.

Hanford, Savannah, Fernald, Rocky Flats: the four biggest
weapons plants in the United States. Three Mile Island and Chernobyl. Rancho Seco and Shoreham. The devastating idea of national sacrifice zones. We must move the world beyond these large
mistakes. Environmentalists, politicians, business leaders, and
citizens—all play an important part in the environmental masquerade.

Given the legacy of our trust in nature, it is hard to think of
anything more timely than the notion of pragmatic forgiveness, of
moving beyond blame. Many may turn away from this concept,
claiming it, too, is naïve considering our environmental predicament. But we do not advocate ignoring issues of responsibility.
Instead, we are calling for an active state of mind—a readiness—
that allows us to move beyond name-calling, entrenchment, and
self-defeat.

Part Two

Present Predicaments

Chapter 3

A Global Greenhouse: Framing the Debate

A person would be an economic fool to put money into a redwood seedling when so many more profitable opportunities are at hand.

—GARRETT HARDIN,
Professor of Ecology, University of California–Santa Barbara

Six of the hottest years on record occurred in the 1980s.

As much energy leaks through American windows every year as flows through the Alaskan pipeline.

Tropical rain forests the size of the city of Philadelphia disappear every week.

These facts are linked by a common thread: global warming.[1] This issue has captured the attention of government, industry, and private citizens alike, for the threat appears as dire and dramatic as the warnings of the Old Testament prophets. The record heat and drought of 1988 was the critical turning point in capturing the general public's attention; it forced some business leaders to recognize that the industrial world's long-standing dependence on fossil fuels and the consequent production of carbon dioxide, are changing the world's ability to regulate temperatures and sustain life. Industrial activity is indeed altering the face of the earth in ways far more consequential than most radical environmentalists dreamt possible in the 1960s and 1970s.[2]

The National Academy of Sciences in 1979 estimated that a doubling of carbon dioxide concentrations above preindustrial levels would raise the earth's temperature between 2.1° and 8.1° F.[3] Within six years of this prediction, three major worldwide associations of scientists reconfirmed the seriousness of these estimates, including the International Council of Scientific Unions, the United Nations Environmental Program, and the prestigious World Meteorological Organization.

These groups all cautioned that such increases in temperature would alter the global availability of water, which could cause widespread disruptions along coastal shorelines and in international agricultural yields. The Environmental Protection Agency further cautions that if present trends continue, the climate may change as fast in the next century as it has over the eighteen thousand years since the last ice age. Here in the United States, global warming could drastically change lives, transforming lush fields of grain into deserts while causing widespread flooding elsewhere. America, and the rest of the world, may be forced by these changes to spawn a revolution in energy generation and consumption, as well as in product design and manufacturing.

The global-warming crisis underscores the delicate balance that exists between industrial growth and environmental health. In order for society to be sustained, significant reductions in emissions of greenhouse gases—primarily carbon dioxide (CO_2) but also chlorofluorocarbons (CFCs) and methane—must occur. The least disruptive way to do this is through greater energy efficiency.

If we don't respond, what might tomorrow feel like? The answer lies in any greenhouse when all of its windows and vents are shut. Transparent windows allow the sun's rays to enter and warm the surroundings, but do not allow the hot air to escape. (Heat is a form of infrared radiation, invisible but felt by the skin. The same window that lets visible light enter, also prevents infrared radiation from escaping. Thus, the temperature rises.) The earth's atmosphere is similar to that of a greenhouse. The atmosphere allows visible light to enter, but blocks infrared rays. Overall, this is beneficial: gases and vapors surround the earth like a blanket, maintaining a warm, inviting atmosphere in which life can flourish. This blanket separates the earth from its cold, empty surroundings. Without a greenhouse blanket, the surface of the earth would be 70° F colder, and the oceans would freeze.

The new problem is "runaway greenhouse," a kind of smothering in our own blanket. A trend toward warming on a worldwide basis cannot easily be halted once it has started. To reverse this is as difficult as warming an ocean, or changing a season. We can only slow the trend down, and hope that the earth's plants and animals adapt to such temperature changes on a grand but gradual basis. This, without a doubt, will demand massive changes in the daily life of humankind.

War Without Borders

In Shakespeare's *Macbeth,* the witches claim that Macbeth's ambitions and pride will continue to rule until the forests move. Macbeth's downfall occurs when an approaching army cuts down the trees of a nearby forest and, using them as camouflage, moves the forest closer and closer to Macbeth's castle. They take the arrogant Macbeth by surprise when they emerge to strike from close range.

In a sense, the modern industrial world has been reliving Macbeth's tragic blindness. Forests are moving. A recent EPA report on global warming shows how this accelerated relocation of resources does not respect man-made political boundaries or ambitions.

After the last ice age, oak trees migrated northward from the southeastern United States as glaciers receded. Temperatures rose slowly enough that forests could adapt to climate changes (forests in these regions have historically moved only sixty miles in a century). The EPA warns, however, that hemlock and sugar maple ranges could move as much as four hundred miles north by the year 2050, most likely causing these classic trees to be pushed to near-extinction in the United States. The financial effects of this forecast are critical: many agricultural and forest products of America's fertile crescent—the Great Plains corridor—may move north to Canada, perhaps carrying billions of dollars in economic dislocation with it.

In California, the sea-level rise induced by high temperatures and melting glaciers would flood much of the Central Valley. Thousands of acres of the world's most prized farmland would be reduced to nonproductive shallow ponds and spillways. The increased salinity of the water would greatly reduce the populations of magnificent white egrets, trumpeter swans, and great blue herons, which depend on freshwater marshes. Regional harvests of crops such as sugar beets and corn, according to EPA models, could be reduced by twenty to forty percent.

Global warming's worsening of air quality would be dramatic. Ozone levels in the San Francisco Bay would triple those of today, which are already in excess of EPA standards.

In Greater Miami, climate change could require at least a half-billion-dollar investment for retrofits and dikes to protect the area's freshwater drinking supplies, roads, airports, and waste-treatment systems from the potential sea rise. The nearby Everglades National Park would be severely threatened, also.

Global warming would aggravate existing beach erosion in Florida and throughout the East Coast. The U.S. Army Corps of Engineers already considers two thousand miles of beach to be in critical condition, at a time when half of the ten thousand miles of shoreline in the lower forty-eight states is under some sort of proposed development. These shoreline investments may suffer serious declines in value if global warming strips away our beaches.[4]

In the Tennessee Valley and lands located within the river basins of the Chattahoochee and Apalachicola rivers, the EPA predicts that between ten and fifty percent of agricultural acreage could become unusable. In many cases, such declines will create economic dislocation in already depressed areas. In the Southeast, for instance, which presently supplies roughly half of America's softwood and hardwood, significant dieback in timber could occur as early as 2020, wrecking local economies.

Studies also note a likely increase in U.S. human mortality. The cities most affected would be New York City, Chicago, and Philadelphia. The EPA global-warming report states: "In the absence of any acclimatization, total summertime mortality in the United States under conditions of doubled carbon dioxide is estimated to rise from an estimated current 1,156 deaths to 7,402 deaths, with deaths in the elderly (aged 65 or over) subset contributing about 70 percent of each figure (727 and 4,605 respectively). Currently, the percentage of elderly in the U.S. is increasing. Thus, the number of mortalities estimated to result from climate change may be larger."[5]

COST OF PLACING SAND ON U.S. RECREATIONAL BEACHES AND
COASTAL BARRIER ISLANDS AND SPITS (IN MILLIONS OF
DOLLARS)

State	Sea Level Rise by 2100			
	Baseline	50 cm	100 cm	200 cm
Maine	22.8	119.4	216.8	412.2
New Hampshire	8.1	38.9	73.4	142.0
Massachusetts	168.4	489.5	841.6	1545.8
Rhode Island	16.3	92.0	160.6	298.2
Connecticut	101.7	516.4	944.1	1799.5
New York	143.6	769.6	1373.6	2581.4
New Jersey	157.6	902.1	1733.3	3492.5
Delaware	4.8	33.6	71.1	161.8
Maryland	5.7	34.5	83.3	212.8
Virginia	30.4	200.8	386.5	798.0
North Carolina	137.4	655.7	1271.2	3240.4
South Carolina	183.5	1157.9	2147.7	4347.7
Georgia	25.9	153.6	262.6	640.3
Florida (Atlantic coast)	120.1	786.6	1791.0	7745.5
Florida (Gulf coast)	149.4	904.3	1688.4	4091.6
Alabama	11.0	59.0	105.3	259.6
Mississippi	13.4	71.9	128.3	369.5
Louisiana	1955.8	2623.1	3492.7	5231.7
Texas	349.6	4188.3	8489.7	17608.3
California	35.7	174.1	324.3	625.7
Oregon	21.9	60.5	152.5	336.3
Washington	51.6	143.0	360.1	794.4
Hawaii	73.5	337.6	646.9	1267.5
Nation	3788.0	14512.0	26745.0	58002.0

Source: Leatherman for U.S. Environmental Protection Agency

The sensible response to the challenge is clear. To avoid the losses, America must get off its petrochemical treadmill.[6] This means less oil, less coal, less waste.

Perhaps one of the most dramatic symbols of human arrogance toward the world's resources and a modern nation's need for energy security is Exxon's Epcot Pavilion in Orlando, Florida. A favorite tourist attraction for millions of people all over the world, Exxon's impressive display actually damns the human race.

Tourists are channeled into carriages "driven through time," starting with panoramic views of our favorite family dinosaurs. To add authenticity, visitors are informed that the smell of the prehistoric swamp that pervades the setting is a petrochemical developed by Exxon and manufactured exclusively for this special effect. The plants and dinosaurs, over time, decayed into the oil and coal that are the resources Exxon now utilizes.

As the visitors are shuffled along, they see a tiger—the corporate icon of Exxon—spinning the world by its paw. The subliminal message of the show, *The Universe of Energy,* is that through its clever capture of fossil fuels, Exxon has placed itself above the world. The cynical message of the program is underlined by the firm's breezy appropriation of nonpetrochemical-based fuels. The millions of tourists who view the slick presentation are told that they have been conveyed through this history of hydrocarbons by solar-powered carriages. Ironically, Exxon was the first oil company to abandon solar research in 1982.

Exxon has captured the history of the world as seen through a hydrocarbon lens, a narrow view that needs to be reexamined. Recent estimates show that global warming will not be stabilized until the year 2050, and that even this stabilization will require a fifty-percent reduction in current fossil fuel use.

A more familiar reminder of what we can no longer afford is Exxon's *Valdez* oil spill off the once-pristine Alaskan coast. This event dramatizes the blind trust in nature which still guides energy policies. Whether or not Joe Hazelwood, captain of the *Valdez,* was drunk when his ship crashed into Bligh Reef is not the real issue. The real issue is affordability.

On Friday, March 24, 1989, only four minutes after midnight, the Exxon *Valdez,* having strayed a mile and a half off course, ground its solid bottom over jagged rocks, and ripped multiple holes in its hull. Over 11 million gallons of crude hit the scenic Prince William Sound, just below Valdez, Alaska. This event continues to exact a toll from all of us. Twenty thousand birds—from thirty different species—were lost, including many of the once-familiar yellow-billed loons, which turned nightmarishly black. At least seven hundred Pacific sea otters and dozens of bald eagles also perished. Some wildlife biologists claim the actual fatality numbers may be five times higher. To say that ninety percent of the Kenai Fjords National Park Shoreland has been hit is only to recite a number; the true cost can only be appreciated when one sees the damage along the 240-mile coastline.

Captain Joseph Hazelwood's career has been marked by a stubborn streak which echoes the world's faith in fossil fuels. In his college yearbook he inscribed the motto: "It can't happen to me." This statement sums up the blind trust in nature that has governed the oil industry for far too long. The firm's simple arrogance, however disarming, is not new.

During the peak of the oil crisis in 1979, when Exxon posted the largest quarterly profit margin in corporate history—a 248-percent increase—Walter Kaufman, then president of Exxon, visited Cornell University. One individual in the crowd of demonstrators asked Kaufman, "What do you think about the fact that my grandmother in the Bronx can't afford your oil prices?" Kaufman responded: "I see no correlation between what I decide in the corporate boardroom and the fate of your grandmother."

Kaufman was wrong. Global warming shows that corporate decisions are inescapably intertwined with the fate of relatives, of neighboring nations, and of the global greenhouse we all share.[7]

The United States has played the major role in building the greenhouse effect. The reason is indisputable: we consume one-fourth of the world's energy. "People born in the U.S. between now and the year 2000 will give off more carbon dioxide from burning fossil fuels than everyone born in the same time period in Latin America and Africa," notes Michael Totten, an aide to Representative Claudine Schneider. In a sense, our extravagant use of energy *requires* the tragedy of such events as the Exxon *Valdez* oil spill.

Though the energy crisis of the seventies fostered a new conservation ethic that allowed the U.S. economy to grow forty percent without any accompanying increase in energy use, the ratio of energy consumption began to climb again in the first part of 1988. One of the most haunting features of a treadmill is its mesmerizing returns onto itself. We know better, yet we forget, returning again and again to the urge to consume rather than conserve. It's easier to waste and takes a lot less planning. But global warming demands that we move the nation as far off the petrochemical treadmill as technically possible, as soon as possible.

Nonetheless, the federal government slashed conservation budgets throughout the eighties. U.S. efforts pale next to those of our foreign competition. Though the United States consumes seventy-five percent more energy per dollar of gross national product than competitors such as France and Japan, American research-and-development funding for new conservation measures lags behind funding levels in France and Japan, as well as in the United Kingdom and West Germany.[8]

How do we get off the treadmill?[9] The answer is known, yet its recognition will be resisted and delayed.

The age of cheap, clean, and abundant energy supplies is over. Domestic oil production has been on the decline since 1970. The nuclear power industry is nearly at a standstill. New energy possibilities in coal and other fossil fuels promise high prices, delayed deliveries, and considerable environmental risks. If America is to assert a leadership role in developing a new approach to both securing clean energy supplies and mitigating the devastating consequences of global warming, then now is the time to explore new alternatives.

A Great Equalizer

The global warming issue touches everyone and everything on the planet. It has forced people to view the earth in a new light, recognizing that what one does in one's own backyard bears consequences for the rest of society. Both rich and poor feel it.

Ironically, it is the wealthy who may suffer the most. As the earth warms, glaciers will melt, causing sea levels to rise, threatening some of the nation's most coveted coastlines. The EPA estimates that the cumulative costs for protecting our coasts, often home for the wealthy, would reach between $73 billion and $111 billion in 1988 dollars for a one-meter rise by the year 2100. Even with this investment, an area the size of Massachusetts would be lost forever, and our dwindling wetlands would be further reduced by fifty to eighty-two percent.

Of course, dramatic changes in global climate could ruin the fragile, less flexible economies of poorer, less mobile developing countries too. Further draining of world resources may contribute to what economist Robert Heilbroner calls the twenty-first century's special kind of "resource wars."

> I do not raise the specter of international blackmail merely to indulge in the dubious sport of shocking the reader. It must be evident that competition for resources may also lead to aggression in the other "normal" direction—that is, aggression by the rich nations against the poor. Yet two considerations give new credibility to nuclear terrorism: nuclear weaponry for the first time makes such actions possible; and "wars of redistribution" may be the only way by which the poor nations can hope to remedy their condition.[10]

Since global warming could actually help some countries by improving regional climates for food production, such "resource wars" could disrupt any coordinated international strategy to combat the larger costs of climatic change. Nevertheless, this issue clearly requires international cooperation. To appreciate the international sensitivities of this issue, consider the following figures.

A study prepared by the Palo Alto–based Electric Power Research Institute notes that twenty-five percent of the world's population resides within industrial societies which consume about seventy-five percent of the world's electricity. Average use of a refrigerator, air conditioner, and heater already has the typical Westerner using nine times as much electricity as the typical resident of the developing world.

The implications of these simple statistics are intertwined with another key factor contributing to the greenhouse effect: the massive destruction of rain forests. The photosynthetic process of trees and all living plants absorbs the carbon dioxide that is released into the air with the burning of fossil fuels. This natural recycling process is being disrupted by countries such as Brazil, current home to a third of the world's rain forest. Burdened with huge debts to world banks, Brazil is converting vast stretches of their forest into instant moneymaking ventures such as short-term cattle farms for American-based fast-food restaurants. The land proves useless after several grazing seasons, and the cattle farmers move on.

In their wake lies the destruction of countless sensitive ecosystems. Although the world's rain forests cover only two percent of the earth's surface, these rich forests contain half of all species of life on the planet. At present, forty-eight species of plant and animal life become extinct every day.

It is estimated that worldwide net tree loss accounts for twenty-five percent of global CO_2 emissions. (Trees that are burned not only no longer absorb carbon dioxide; in the process of burning, they release more of it into the atmosphere.) Adding to the dilemma is the fact that almost half of the world's population depends on firewood for cooking and home heating. As areas around the globe become developed, they will switch to electricity, which will partially arrest the deterioration of this element in the current global-warming equation. But this is likely to increase the use of fossil fuels to produce electricity. If the entire world used as much electricity per capita as the industrial world uses now, worldwide use of electricity would be at least three times as great. Such catch-22 scenarios help show why the fossil-fuel addiction seems impossible to break: the more dependent we become on oil, the harder it is to secure an alternative route.

Deforestation is hardly an issue confined to foreign borders. High demand from other countries for U.S. timber, and the notoriously weakened dollar, have created a domestic timber industry boom at the expense of regal old-growth giants in Oregon. Critics claim the U.S. Forest Service is caving in to the Pacific Northwest's logging industry, which sells massive stretches of American forest to Japanese consumers.

Coupled with increases in the use of fossil fuels over the last one hundred years, global deforestation has already led to a doubling of carbon dioxide in our atmosphere. In light of this, we must face the question: How can we balance our world's need for energy with these urgent environmental concerns? To date, this question has not been adequately addressed by any government.

A December 1988 report by the Electric Power Research Institute predicts that, because of its abundance, coal will supply about two-thirds of the additional energy needed worldwide over the next fifty years. This report advocates the development of an innovative clean coal technology program, and asserts that the domestic electric utility industry will invest more than $3 billion to make this program a reality. This program received a push from the federal government back in 1986 in light of Canada's concerns about acid rain resulting from U.S.-burned coal.[11]

This move toward less coal emissions is welcome, but America and its neighbors—as well as coal advocates in China and India—have to move beyond coal, and beyond other fossil fuels. To continue to rely on coal consumption, without seeking safer replacements, is like tap-dancing on thin ice. Consider the following observations by Dean Abrahamson, from a speech he gave at the Hubert H. Humphrey Institute of Public Affairs at the University of Minnesota:

> There is little hope for slowing climatic change if new commitments continue to be made to coal and the other hydrocarbons. Yet coal is expected to surpass petroleum as the world's most utilized fuel between now and the middle of the next century. So-called clean coal technology, the deployment of which would increase greenhouse gas emissions, is now slated to receive a public dole of over $500 million of federal funds for the 1990 fiscal year. Continued subsidies of coal, the most environmentally noxious of the fossil fuels, and of the destruction of old-growth forests are among the considerations which led to the following observation by D. A. Wirth in *Foreign Policy:* "the implications of the greenhouse phenomenon have not played the slightest role in long-term strategic planning by the U.S. government."

This shift away from coal and oil won't be easy. Projections by the World Energy Conference's Conservation Commission say that the amount of fossil fuels used in the year 2060 will be 1.64

times the present volume.[12] Since this assumes that hydropower increases by five times and nuclear by eighteen times—the latter assumption being quite debatable—the reliance on fossil fuels could even be greater. Our search for safer and more cost-effective energy substitutes will be hampered.

In addition, the forecasted increase in the use of coal has fostered bizarre and costly options to treat the resulting gases. Many options rely on technologies that profitably exploit one part of the environment to save another. For instance, one proposal calls for the pumping of carbon dioxide into pipelines leading to reservoirs deep in the ocean. Though this option—cross-stitching both American coasts with miles of heavy-duty piping in corrosive salt waters—may be technically possible, it means spending billions of dollars pursuing high-tech glamour instead of reasonable and appropriate answers. Such an effort is the equivalent to our misplaced faith in the onetime promise of "too-cheap-to-meter" nuclear power. America can no longer afford to be distracted by the lure of unneeded[13] or damaging[14] energy technologies.

The hard-won path toward greater energy efficiency and environmentally sound policies will have greatest impact on the developing nations. With far fewer financial resources than the United States, they are going to have to upgrade their practices faster than the industrialized world.

Promising steps in the recognition of the need for international cooperation is the Declaration of the Hague, which the World Watch Institute has described as "an environmental security council." Countries as diverse as West Germany, Pakistan, and Hungary had signed an agreement by 1990 to finance the transfer of energy-efficient technologies and CFC substitutes to the developing world in exchange for the recipients' reducing carbon dioxide and CFC emissions.

Ironically, the three largest emitters of carbon dioxide—China, the United States, and the Soviet Union—were not invited because of their known reluctance to sign such agreements. Nevertheless, China has, despite some formidable challenges ahead, demonstrated the potential for reducing energy intensity. (Energy intensity is a measurement of the amount of energy consumed per unit of economic output.) Since 1979, China has cut its energy intensity by four percent per year. Another glimmer of hope is that the Soviet Union, by improving efficiency, and by pursuing structural reforms through perestroika, could limit its greenhouse-gas emissions at no extra cost to the Soviet economy.[15]

Japan could take the lead in helping developing nations tackle environmental problems. While America played the role of the great provider in the twentieth century, Japan, together with the "little dragons" along the Pacific Rim, is today a logical leader in dispersing foreign aid and reaping the benefits of such investments.

Within this larger context of a world market working to promote environmental restoration, the expense of efficiency controls takes on a new aspect—that of a timely, diplomatic investment to improve national and global security.

Who Are the Economic Fools?

Walt Whitman celebrates the cutting down of redwood trees in his poem "Song of the Redwood Tree," and the glory he finds in the sound of saws once again reminds us what is wrong with America's estimate of nature.[16] Garrett Hardin takes this point further, sardonically arguing that one would be an economic fool to plant a redwood tree because it takes so long—some two thousand years—for a redwood to reach its full value under today's standard assumptions.

But this belief that "nature is nothing in itself until divinely serviceable by man" makes Whitman's generation the ultimate economic fools. Regrettably, most political and business leaders still glorify the chopping down of natural resources for conversion into quick and easy profits. To level forests is not an adequate celebration of what Whitman called "the rising, teeming stature of humanity," because disappearing forests are now costing all of us. Hardin's calculation of the $14,000 value of a redwood tree after two thousand years also fails to include the environmental benefits inherent in one tree's contribution to mitigating the greenhouse effect.

U.S. AID forester Michael Benge has been trying to prove the value of another particular tree—the wild tamarind—in order to save rain forests. A fast-growing member of the legume family, this tree is nitrogen-fixing, so it enriches soil as it also serves as fence, firewood, and food for livestock. This tree can help replenish the soil while serving other commercial uses because of its fast rate of growth. The world could invest in these safer alternatives. It is the international banks, dictating development policies for most of the world, that should prove the most critical player in halting this maddening pace of deforestation.[17]

How much are environmental benefits, such as those provided by trees, actually worth? Throughout the world, experts are now scrambling to quantify the real environmental economic costs associated with energy production and greater efficiency in order to move the nation beyond the "time discount" preoccupation of modern economic thinking. This concept postulates that present consumption reaps greater value than preservation of resources for future use. This assumption, which has guided thinkers from Adam Smith and John Locke to most modern-day supply-side economists, is one cause of today's environmental crisis.

Businesspeople such as Roger Sant of Applied Energy Services, Inc., have taken it upon themselves to prove the economic value of forests. Because Sant—an independent power generator—is now constructing a coal-fired plant in Uncasville, Connecticut, he is paying to help plant 52 million trees in Guatemala. These trees are expected to absorb 15 million tons of carbon dioxide over forty years, the same amount expected to be emitted by his power plant.

Sant, who is also chair of the Washington, D.C.–based Environmental and Energy Institute, claims that he will include reforestation projects for every new coal plant his firm constructs. "Energy policy ought to be seen through a greenhouse lens. That ought to be a principal focus," says Sant, adding that utilities and independent power producers should take a leadership role on global warming by stressing energy efficiency and conservation in every move they make.

Reforestation efforts are also building on several fronts. A plan by the World Resources Institute, also backed by the World Bank and the United Nations, promises to invest $8 billion over five years to plant trees. In Thailand and India, Buddhists are recognizing ecological values in their beliefs, and promoting sizable tree planting campaigns. In the United States, researchers at Lawrence

Berkeley Laboratory have discovered a way to utilize trees, along with white paint, to help mitigate the magnification of temperatures in urban centers, known as "the heat-island effect." (For example, since 1940, Los Angeles temperatures have increased by 5° F.)

Long before homes were cooled by air conditioners, trees were planted and outside walls painted white to achieve the same effect. Computer models verify that a return to this approach is a most economical way to combat global warming. What is so satisfying about urban trees is that their aesthetic value is matched by their practical value. They improve the local climate and, by serving as shade and windbreak, reduce the loss of moisture from soil. Trees are remarkably effective in cooling buildings in summer, at around one one-hundredth of what it would cost to get an equivalent amount of cooling from power plants and air-conditioning equipment. On hot summer days, a tree can act as a natural "evaporative cooler" using up to one hundred gallons of water a day, thus lowering the ambient temperature of otherwise scorching city streets. Anyone who has sweated out an August in Manhattan or a summer in Phoenix may now ask: Would we not be economic fools if we keep our cities treeless?

In addition to saving energy, urban trees and light-colored surfaces are probably the least expensive way to decrease carbon dioxide emissions. By reducing the need to burn fossil fuels for power, these old-fashioned tools carry many indirect benefits that the last several generations seem to have forgotten.

Here is the global warming reduction recipe the Lawrence Berkeley Lab (LBL) now suggests for each citizen: Pay $15 to $50 to plant and water three trees around a house, wait ten years for the trees to grow, and then save about 1 or 2 kilowatts of peak power and about 750 to 2000 kilowatt-hours per year in air-conditioning energy per house—a value of $50 to $150 each year. Similarly, when asphalt streets or parking lots need resurfacing, they should be finished off with a thin surface of white sand, and any reroofing jobs should be done in white.

Trees can also reduce heating bills by thirty percent. And LBL's supply-curve models have shown that trees could help eliminate much of Los Angeles's smog problem.

The Lawrence Berkeley Lab, led by conservation guru Art Rosenfeld, thinks big, and their goals are quite honorable: to reduce energy intensity by 3.5 percent over the next twenty years. If we followed their route, America could keep its energy usage at current levels and save from $1.3 to 2.2 trillion (in 1987 dollars).[18] The fundamental message is clear. We can tackle the challenge of global warming, and improve America's industrial edge in the process.

This is how LBL summarizes the benefits of its recommendations: "Investments in improved efficiency would provide U.S. industry with a better competitive position in world markets, and free up more than $100 billion annually for capital investments in other U.S. industries. The poor would benefit from lower energy costs and additional jobs. Reduced emissions of carbon dioxide and other pollutants would lessen environmental damage and reduce the impact of global warming."

Steven Schneider, a climate expert at the National Center for Atmospheric Research, calls this approach a "tie-in strategy," since it would enable Americans to reduce the trade deficit, enhance competitiveness, free up capital for research, and reduce greenhouse gases all at once.

A recent U.S. Department of Energy report echoes many of LBL's findings, noting that through energy conservation measures, the United States could stave off a projected thirty-eight-percent rise in carbon dioxide emissions by the year 2010. This same DOE report underscores the fact that what is needed is a global response to the greenhouse effect, one that entices multinationals to get off the petrochemical treadmill as much as possible.[19] Even if the United States reduces its emissions of carbon dioxide to 1985 levels, however, global levels would only decrease seven percent, without similar efforts by other nations.

At present, the tilted playing field that favors the production of more fossil-fuel–based energy over conservation is common around the globe. In many planned economies and the developing world, it is business as usual to subsidize fossil-fuel supply and dismiss efficiency demands. A striking image of the inadequacy of some nations' energy policies, in spite of China's overall gains in reducing energy use, comes from Beijing. Even though winters in

Beijing are as cold as in Boston, brand-new buildings are uninsulated and are heated by heavily subsidized coal burning.

Less Is More

The discovery that conservation is a resource is a clear demonstration of the principle of "Less is more." The oil crisis of the seventies began this revolution, spurring the first generation of efficiency reforms and product-design innovations. The second wave of innovations, propelled by what might be called the second oil crisis—the *Valdez* spill—will need the helping hand of government to further sharpen the tools we already have.

Consider the following facts: Any person can "produce" energy by using light bulbs that use one-fourth as much energy as standard bulbs. Houses, through use of new insulations, can cut energy use by nine-tenths.

Ironically, in the absence of strong federal leadership on energy, states have played the critical roles in implementing energy conservation and efficiency programs. The New England Power Service Company has a remarkably advanced state conservation program. In 1989, the company spent $40 million to install energy-efficient lights, insulate water heaters, and improve industrial efficiency throughout its service area. By 1991, the utility hopes to displace 100,000 tons of coal by way of this program. Over the fifteen-year planning horizon, the savings will equate to one-third of the utility's energy requirements.

Another forward-looking state effort comes from the New York State Energy Research and Development Authority, which was formed in 1975 as a public-benefit corporation mandated to fund alternative energy concepts. A good example is NYSERDA's many district heating and cooling programs. Many of the older heating systems in American cities are extremely inefficient and waste vast quantities of energy. Comparing the old systems to the new is a little like comparing a Model T to a 1990 Celica. Jamestown, Rochester, and Buffalo are current success stories, as these communities now save between twenty and forty-five percent of past energy bills. Not only do these upgrades improve air quality, they also serve as economic-development boons.[20]

New York was also one of the first states to recognize that

CHANGING PATTERNS IN THE USE OF ENERGY RESOURCES IN THE UNITED STATES

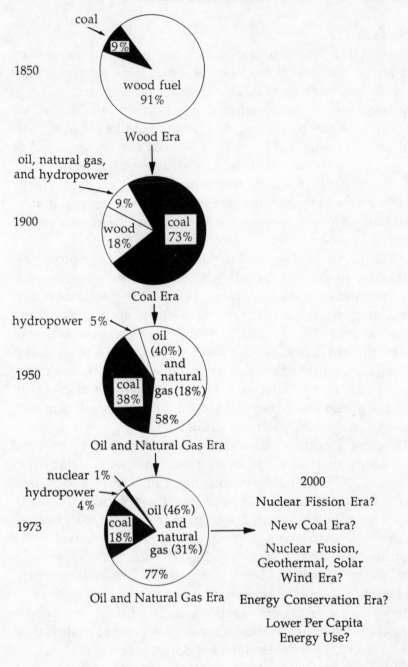

Source: U.S. Bureau of Census
and Resources for the Future

capturing heat produced in industrial processes for reuse as energy was a sensible idea. In doing so, New York and other states proved many old-school planners wrong: developing more centralized energy generation is not always incompatible with the soft energy path of increased efficiency and recycling.[21]

"Less is more" programs have also been developed on the West Coast. California's adoption of standards for the single largest user of electricity in the home—the refrigerator—forced national manufacturers to create greater efficiencies, which in turn became de facto industry benchmarks. Such refrigerator standards could allow the United States to avoid doubling its nuclear power-plant fleet. California has also been a leader in developing renewable energy supplies, cutting its reliance on fossil-fueled power plants from eighty percent in the midseventies to almost half of that today.

States took the lead in innovative energy programs because of the lack of any high-visibility energy policy being staked out at the White House. The emerging environmental consequences attendant upon future energy choices, however, will command a revival of federal responsibility in the 1990s. A replacement for the petrochemical treadmill cannot be built by states alone.

One federal agency that has played a leadership role in promoting a more efficient use of existing resources is the Bonneville Power Administration (BPA), which was created in 1937 to provide cheap power throughout the Pacific Northwest by marketing the tremendous energy potential of the magnificent Columbia River. Thirty different federal dams are part of the system.

A sample accomplishment of the BPA is its promotion of the idea of "least-cost" energy planning. By initiating innovative conservation efforts, such as the investing of $21 million to retrofit more than ninety percent of the entire community of Hood River, BPA is breaking new ground. They not only quantify what energy savings can be achieved, but also analyze how their approach can be marketed to other communities across the United States.

By better coordinating its activities with Canada's B.C. Hydro—which built U.S.–financed dams under a special treaty in the 1960s—BPA has captured an additional 600 megawatts of power, some of which is now being marketed to California on an experimental basis. This is the equivalent of one nuclear reactor's worth of power, but it did not require one bucketful of cement. Furthermore, BPA has negotiated a trend-setting contract with Southern California Edison, which serves the Los Angeles basin, whereby the two parties exchange power to take advantage of each other's energy peaks and demands without contributing to "the air quality problems of Southern California or the greenhouse effect," notes BPA's deputy administrator, Jack Robertson.

"If the West Coast was better able to integrate utility systems, there could be 5,000 to 6,000 megawatts of additional power that could be achieved by squeezing the existing systems and using integration and interregional energy transfers as resources," Robertson added. "Instead of building more nuclear and coal plants, we should build much less costly reinforcement of transmission links, allowing for transfers of energy back and forth. This upgrade should be part of our national energy plan.

One way to entice the entire United States to become more energy-efficient would be to establish a "golf score" for utilities. Under a system proposed by David Moskovitz, former utility commissioner of the state of Maine, a utility's score would equal the cost of serving its average residential or commercial customer. As in the game of golf—where the lower score is better—utilities would compete with one another on the basis of efficiency, not power generation. Tying profits to an index of average regional customer bills would provide incentives for supply-side efficiency improvements and would reduce pollution. Under these rewritten profit rules, utilities could increase revenues by selling energy services—such as better windows and light bulbs.

All eyes are on America to determine how far it can go with a second generation of efficiency enhancements. All told, Americans already save $150 billion per year because of reduced oil consumption fostered by improvements in cars, buildings, and manufactories since 1973. Without the first generation of these improvements, the carbon dioxide feeding global warming would be fifty percent worse. Moreover, our trade deficit would have slipped another $50 billion into the red.[22]

Winning the War

The Global End-Use Oriented Energy Project asserts that it is indeed possible to hold energy use constant while reducing carbon dioxide over the next fifty years, even as the world population doubles and gross world product quadruples.

Meeting these goals will require a national energy policy. Will President Bush, a former Texas oilman, take the responsible path toward national security by following the lead of such states as California or New York, or will he follow the path of least resistance and continue to blindly embrace our past mistakes?

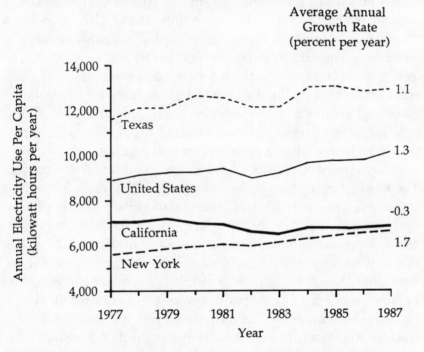

PER CAPITA ELECTRICITY USE IN CALIFORNIA, NEW YORK, TEXAS, AND THE UNITED STATES, 1977–1987

Source: Robert J. Mowris, Lawrence Berkeley Laboratory; U.S. Energy Information Agency, *Electric Power Annual* (1982, 1987), U. S. Department of Commerce, *U. S. Statistical Abstract of the United States* (1985, 1989).

If Texas is any indication, we have reason for deep concern. Texas represents the ultimate in Big Oil mentality. It is the only state in the lower forty-eight that restricts sales of excess energy to its neighboring states, and instead blindly plans for more and more generation and consumption. In fact, utilities actively market excessive consumption from unneeded new nuclear power units. Texas's energy use is projected to rise for the next ten years, while most states strive for gains in efficiency.[23]

Congress can help, by dragging reluctant states into the age of efficiency. Already leaders from both parties have announced new federal initiatives on energy policy. Senator Tim Wirth of Colorado and Congresswoman Claudine Schneider of Rhode Island have both introduced bills calling for three-year increases of research and development funding in the area of energy efficiency and renewable energy. The Wirth bill would also establish a "Least-Cost National Energy Plan" which would mandate a twenty-percent carbon dioxide reduction by the year 2000. The legislation stipulates that the top two R&D priorities of the federal Department of Energy should be a reduction in greenhouse gases and greater energy efficiency. Additionally, it calls for the establishment of regional centers for industrial efficiency, important links in revitalizing American manufacturing.

But government does not have all the resources to do the job. Therefore, partnerships between business and government will be necessary. The government's response to global warming has to move toward policies that encourage such partnerships to improve American industry. Marc Ross, a University of Michigan physicist who serves as a consultant to the Department of Energy, highlights the challenge: "It will take government intervention because there are so many players here. You have over 80 million households using appliances. You have 100,000 to 200,000 contractors who have to learn how to better insulate houses."

Ross has identified five areas where government initiative can help ease global warming over the next two decades: conservation; process changes; fuel switching to natural gas; greater reliance on electricity and biomass; and recycling. The good news is that these goals can be achieved without much government money.

Efforts to reverse deforestation and improve efficiency, as well as manufacturing reforms, are just a few links in a long list of new measures that have to be adopted and reinforced on a worldwide basis to combat global warming. The critical player in securing environmental excellence is government. Luckily, joint ventures between governments, private industry, and utilities are financing ways to discover energy answers. The chief challenge before us now is how to shorten the time it takes to discover an answer, and then make it readily available in the marketplace. This lesson applies not only to efficiency innovations, but to the next step as well: new technologies.

In the development of new power-generation hardware such as a better gas turbine, a site-specific demonstration is typically co-funded by a governmental financing authority and perhaps another utility or entrepreneur. If the product demonstration is a success and generates sufficient interest, it is followed by the dispersal of the product within an industrial group.

The typical time for the completion of this cycle in the United States is fifteen years: roughly five years of design, five of development, and five of dissemination. (In Japan, due to the long-term focus of government-industry R&D efforts, this time frame has been shortened on the average to a total of five years.) In light of the current environmental crisis and increasing foreign competition, America needs to speed up this cycle by linking energy goals with environmental needs and economy savings from the start.

According to Robert Williams of Princeton's Center for Energy and Environmental Studies, developing countries could benefit from extensive military R&D on jet turbines with a series of added innovations to adapt such engines for power generation. From a global warming perspective, these turbines are particularly beneficial if they are wedded to biomass energy supplies.[24]

The use of organic matter such as trees and plants—referred to as "biomass fuel"—combats the greenhouse effect. This is achieved in three important ways: by replacing fossil fuel with biofuels; by sequestering carbon dioxide already in the atmosphere in tree plantations; and by reducing deforestation and the resulting release of carbon dioxide by giving nations reasons to recognize the value of properly managed tree plantations.

Biomass currently accounts for thirty-six percent of the world's energy, but is used very inefficiently. Its use makes inherent sense in the developing world, especially in conjunction with new efficient turbines. New innovations that recycle steam and thus recapture energy previously lost make these machines adaptable to the modest economies of many developing countries. These modified jet turbines are not yet commercially available, but, in a strange twist of fate, coal R&D may provide the needed final push. Hundreds of millions of public and private expenditures in the United States, Western Europe, and Japan have resulted in major advances in the technology of firing high-efficiency, low-cost gas turbines with gas derived from coal. Much of this coal-gasification turbine research and development is directly relevant to biomass, notes Williams. Because biomass does not have the sulfur problem associated with coal use, running such turbines on biomass is cleaner and cheaper. This is an important ground for hope. The developing world can avoid the treadmill, with a little help from friends in the research community.

There are a few cases where government and private industry working together have achieved R&D successes that promise an easing of the global-warming phenomenon. One of these is the giant LUZ International solar thermal farm in California's desolate Mojave Desert, where 650,000 parabolic mirrors stretch over one thousand acres, producing ninety-five percent of the world's solar electricity.

By mid-decade, farms like these will be generating a total of 600 megawatts. That is enough power to supply more than 300,000 homes. In addition, each 80-megawatt solar plant saves 325 millions pounds of carbon dioxide emissions which would be given off by any fossil-fuel plant producing the same amount of energy.

LUZ, an Israeli–U.S. joint venture, moved to California in 1983 to take advantage of federal and state solar tax credits and independent power contracts.[25] The credits and contracts provided a subsidy sufficient to help get LUZ's fledgling "parabolic trough" technology out of the laboratory and into the steady sun of southeastern California.

LUZ's technology tracks the sun with microprocessors as it moves from horizon to horizon, capturing heat to raise the temperature of the generating fluids. A heat exchanger then transmits this heat to turn a traditional turbine (which also runs on natural gas when sunlight is insufficient), allowing the farms to generate electricity to sell to utilities. LUZ is currently working on a research project with the California Energy Commission to increase the efficiency of the "parabolic trough" by eliminating a transfer loop from the process. This would eliminate a potential waste problem, as water would replace oil as the heat-transfer fluid.

In every solution to the energy dilemma, whether it is new efficient turbines, parabolic troughs, least-cost plans, or centers for industrial efficiency, government has a role. Its key role, beneath all the contracting details, is as an enabler, helping industry to develop its alternatives. By 1986, states as diverse as California, Idaho, and Maine had been able to defer their needs for new coal and nuclear plants by acquiring 1,424 independent power projects utilizing alternate resources such as solar, wind, and hydro energy. These alternative projects average a capacity of just 12 megawatts, but demonstrate how public-private partnerships are helping to solve environmental dilemmas. In the overall scheme of things, such small incremental power additions make more sense than massive new plants. Dozens of unfinished nuclear power plants across America stand as unfortunate reminders of this fact.

Small, independent applications of alternative energy sources are universally acknowledged by the research community to be influential and eminently productive in mitigating global warming. We can no longer afford to consider these operating alternatives the gadgets of hippies and technocrats. In light of government's tight pocketbook, these new power projects represent the vanguard of a society more in tune with the limits and organic rhythms of the earth. They are the machines by which we can build more affordable beliefs, more sustaining lifestyles.

Chapter 4

On the Local Front: A Citizen's Guide

Although few would care to admit it, many of the problems as-sociated with technology are the result of the use of machines by the masses. Environmental pollution, the breakdown of society, and many of the stresses felt by both institutions and individuals are due to the personal use of the automobile, the aerosol can, or the handgun—of the machine. A technological society, after all, is one in which everyone has access to technology.

—WITOLD RYBCZYNSKI

Technology helps us to explore new realms and, by rapid incre-ments, to advance civilization. We are free to detach ourselves from the tasks associated with the survival of our grandparents. Food gathering is now taken care of by mechanical harvesters. Homes are built not by the hands of friends, but by specialized craftsmen dependent upon forklifts and electrical hammers. And transportation has become an enterprise dominated by individual cars maintained by well-paid mechanics.

Our era's high romance with mechanical appliances best illus-trates how we have fallen in love with gadgetry, rather than with the solving of social problems. No one can seriously dispute that electricity has made life more convenient. Why else would the use of household electrical power have spread from one-sixth of all American families in 1912 to two-thirds by 1927? Nonetheless, promises of how the electric iron and washing machine would create vast amounts of leisure time have since proven false. Many are now spending the same amount of time in the kitchen as before—if not more—trying to read the directions for the latest electronic device.

America's wholehearted embrace of technology, and Western culture's idea that technologies offer ultimate answers to all our woes, has far-reaching consequences. Critics from Henry David Thoreau to Wendell Berry have noted that we have become severed from the traditional belief that answers to human problems depend upon the earth's long-standing rhythms and rules. Home gardens, farming, and self-propelled transport are now exceptions, rather than the rule, of everyday life. For many, it is the rhythm of our cars, the hum of our homes' vast arsenal of electronic aids, that define our day rather than the weather or the needs of the soil. Yet a fuller sense of the earth is resurfacing today, with a stronger suspicion of the rule of sophisticated machines. As E. F. Schumacher once said, "Any third rate engineer or researcher can increase complexity, but it takes a certain flair of real insight to make things simple again."

This return to the earth was once the celebrated chore of only those advanced in training and age. Thoreau went to Walden well after college. Most find their garden during retirement years. Yet today, a discontent with the music of machines and the dizzy complexity of modern technology is taking root at an earlier age.

When a teacher of four-year-olds at the Dandelion Day Care Center in Rochester, New York, asked a classroom what they thought of neighborhood garbage, most children exclaimed that it was "bad stuff." Suddenly one child began to go beyond this initial reaction and ask about a solution. "What do we do if we run out of garbage cans?" This sense of limits is exactly where modern society now finds itself. Another four-year-old suggested that it would take "all day and all night and even more" to clean up the area's rubbish. After further discussion of this ugly topic, one frustrated child rose up and declared, "I would get angry if I had a short temper, or sad if I had a long one."

This poetic line, ignorant of today's grown-up talk about "clean technologies" and "waste minimization," captures the brilliance of youthful immediacy and introspection. They observe the scene and describe it without blinders. Far too often, the qualifying complexities of adult society obscure what is needed. "The young, miserably educated as they are, bring with them almost nothing but healthy instincts," observes Theodore Roszak in the chapter entitled "Technocracy's Children" from his *The Making of a Counter Culture*. He warns that technological society needs to protect this childlike innocence. "The project of building a sophisticated framework of thought atop those instincts is rather like trying to graft an oak tree upon a wildflower. How to sustain an oak tree? More important, how to avoid crushing the wildflower?" Such is the challenge that confronts those of us concerned with environmental reform.

The child's reaction, quoted above, strengthened by the simple beauty of her communication, clarifies the deep dissatisfaction most adults feel when discussing environmental problems. We would prefer that "it" would go away and disappear. We are trained to trust that technology will direct our society's waste to some safe haven somewhere else—a belief we increasingly realize is false.

The dominant members of our culture, writes Roszak, embrace and propagate the trust in technocracy—a social system where problems are solved by ever new and more complex answers—as the "purely neutral umpire in an athletic contest." Given the stakes in the contest, namely quality of life, we should more fully scrutinize this umpire's rules. At present, technocracy has become somewhat invisible, "as unobtrusively pervasive as the air we breathe," observes Roszak. Though ignored, the umpire "is the most significant figure in the game." After all, technocracy has defined how most of us have envisioned environmental solutions since World War II. Anyone who has worked a week in a successful high-tech firm, or a month in most large government bureaucracies, has felt and obeyed this silencing umpire.

Technocracy is not the answer. Appropriate use of technology is. The glamour associated with increased technology for technology's sake carries less and less weight. The boredom, consumption, and waste that technocracy has fostered and sustained feeds the discontent of ever-increasing numbers of people. What is needed is a delicate blend of the expertise of environmental managers with a childlike urgency for solutions.

While a child's innocence is refreshing, our treatment of children's wastes epitomizes how absurdly insistent machine societies can become in their disregard of the past. Consider this startling fact: today's child requires up to ten thousand diapers before adjusting to the wonders of toilets. All told, ninety-eight percent of America's parents now use disposable diapers for their toddlers and infants. This is just one example of how the United States has become the most wasteful nation in the world. In 1988 alone, approximately 18 billion disposable diapers ended up in bulging and leaking landfills. The cost of collection and disposal of diapers has climbed to $350 million annually and threatens to pollute underground water supplies as well as to spread diseases such as Hepatitis A.

Carl Lehrburger of the New York–based Energy Answers Corporation argues that diapers should be composted. In Europe, over 200 municipal solid-waste compost plants are in operation and diapers do not dampen the public's confidence in composting. To state it sportively: We need a more appropriate diaper, what E. F. Schumacher might call a diaper with human needs in mind.

Developing this more sensible diaper is only one tiny part of the solution to the pollution problem, but it represents a greater point. We have traditionally associated pollution problems with the oil refinery at the edge of town, or the brown haze that descends on the city in the heat of summer. Some of the biggest threats to your health, however, lie under the kitchen sink, under the hood of your car, or in your backyard. Since people in modern, industrial societies spend roughly ninety percent of their time indoors, the most direct health consequences for you probably reside in your own home and workplace. This doesn't mean, of course, that we should ignore the global environmental threats that affect us all. What it does mean is that you, too, are a part of the answer. After all, the typical American spends roughly sixty-six percent of his or her income on the following: the home (thirty percent), transportation (eighteen percent), and food (eighteen percent). All of these expenditures—the choices we make—affect the environment directly. Fortunately, they also identify the most important paths for substantial environmental reform.

Your Home

The link between your home and your concerns over the greenhouse effect is your daily use of energy. Minute by minute, the spin of your utility dial directs our environmental destiny. To appreciate the astonishing impact homeowners can make, one should look to Sweden, where the average energy use for home heating is only two-thirds that of other European and North American countries. What's more impressive is that the Swedes have accomplished this while enjoying higher average indoor temperatures, despite rigorous winters, than any other country in the world.

Faced with a housing shortage after World War II, the Swedish government expanded its housing stock by building more top-quality homes. This initiative resulted in the Million Homes program in the midsixties, which once again demonstrates how governments can stimulate environmental excellence. With a generous home-loan program that penetrated almost the entire housing market, a third of Sweden's homes were built. The program set worldwide standards for construction practices, home financing, building research, and code designs.

Walk into the typical Swedish home and you will notice an immediate contrast to American homes: there are no drafts. Moreover, they sound like recording studios, enriching sounds and the human voice. Walls, floors, and windows are all designed to make such effective use of insulation that air flows must be controlled by a ventilation system. Of special note are Swedish windows, whose initial design dates back to the eleventh century when the world's first windows were mere leather flaps. Today, Swedish windows typically have three panes, sometimes four. Some even contain an inert gas, argon, for added insulation. Exterior doors often have foam-core insulation, multiple weather strippings, and sometimes stainless-steel fittings and multipoint locks. Building codes forbid electrical conduits and plumbing lines from penetrating the polyethylene membrane that serves as an air/vapor lock. As a result of precise building standards, the air exchange ratio occurring naturally in a Swedish house is about half that of a typical new American home and a quarter of that in the U.S. housing stock as a whole.

So little heat escapes from a house built to these strict standards that "free heat," much of it from what Americans call passive-solar designs, can provide over two-thirds of all heating requirements.

The Swedes do not rely on technological gimmicks to achieve such excellence; instead, they integrate simple techniques in housing manufacturing into the overall design and construction of homes. The results are clear. Under the 1984 Swedish standard, whereby fifty percent of the heat must be recovered from the ventilation system, houses use only a quarter of the electricity consumed by the equivalent American home in Minneapolis. This is due in part to the fact that home-building is still practiced as a respected craft in Sweden. Homes are not viewed as short-term speculative capital assets, but rather as permanent sanctuaries. The emphasis on quality is reflected in the government's attention to efficiency, as most developers provide detailed economic information regarding energy-saving features to everyone in the housing market.

Compare this enlightened, integrated approach to home-building with the practices prevalent in the United States.[1] The Veterans Administration issued 60 million home loans between 1980 and 1988. Only 18,000 of these included any energy-efficient components. That is only one out of every 37,000 loans to a group that is well under a quarter of the total population. No wonder we still lose as much energy through our windows as we pump from Alaska.

An additional problem, notes Jim Barron of the New York State Energy Research and Development Authority, is the absence of any serious research and development on America's housing policies. This inaction contrasts sharply with the federal government's support for research in agriculture, an area which shares many characteristics with housing. Both industries contribute about equally to the nation's gross national product, and are composed of tens of thousands of small firms. Federal spending on agriculture, however, outpaces what is spent on housing by a factor of approximately one hundred to one, states Barron. The sizable government expenditures on agriculture have created the most advanced and productive farming techniques in the world, and there is every reason to believe that targeted investments in housing upgrades could bring similar benefits.

"Here in America, our policies on housing have been dominated by concerns over short-term paybacks," remarked Barron.

"There is no recognition that a house represents a seventy-year investment that is costing us billions and billions of dollars in environmental adjustments and lost energy."

It is this recognition of the importance of permanent homes, and the need for standardized measures of excellence, that has shaped the Swedish home-building industry into a refined manufacturing process. It starts when a tree is felled in the forest, and ends in a house factory. Employing a jig rigged to a semiautomatic tilt-table, a single Swedish worker can construct a whole wall section. As the jig moves down the production line, siding or gypsum board is fastened by preprogrammed screw guns which diminish the bulges caused by imperfect nailing. The completed homes are delivered to site and, with the help of a crane and four workers, can be erected in as little as one day. The total time elapsed between buyer's order and occupancy is often only two weeks.

The Swedish financing approach is deliberately designed to minimize the initial cost of energy improvements. The typical house is financed with below-market-rate government loans, which can only be granted with proof of a range of energy-efficiency features. According to an American Council for an Energy Efficient Economy (ACEEE) spokesperson, the "strongest single force" driving Sweden's ninety-percent market penetration of energy-efficiency design features is loan subsidies.

"Sweden's experience indicates no single lesson more strongly than that material progress with new energy-saving housing technologies requires a national commitment of research monies with a well-coordinated, cooperative policy setting," notes an ACEEE report. It astutely recommends that the United States must "reunite residential energy conservation policy and housing policy."[2]

Your Utility

The utilities should be key players in bringing about substantial residential energy upgrades and reforms in the United States. Since they were instrumental in peddling electrical appliances in the first place,[3] it is appropriate that utilities come full circle by bringing environmental excellence back into our homes. The U.S. system of power generation and distribution comes closer than any other sector of our economy to matching the planned-society approach which governs countries such as Sweden. Rather than planning more "load-building" programs designed to increase America's lust for more electricity, the utility of tomorrow should market products that do just the opposite: reduce demand for electricity by stretching existing resources. By developing new product lines featuring efficiency in our homes, they could bring new and unexpected empires.

Your home is the next frontier for utilities because the traditional role of utilities as monolithic producers and sellers of power is about to change. The new, competitive electricity market now relies more on independent producers to generate power, multiple-company agreements to provide "bulk power" transmission, and efficient grid systems to circumvent the need to build new power plants. In order to prosper, utilities must now become leaders in environmental excellence, providing energy services rather than just promoting increased energy consumption. Current utility demand-side management programs are just the beginning of this trend. In the future, utilities will be installing photovoltaic panels on rooftops, marketing better windows, and selling us more efficient lighting, if they care about averting extinction.

An early example of a new utility-environment relationship comes from the Pacific Northwest. Under the leadership of the Bonneville Power Administration (BPA), a federal public agency that mimics a giant utility, the Northwest was divided into three climate zones for its Residential Standards Demonstration Program. Two thousand home-builders became certified Model Conservation Standards (MCS) builders, submitting designs for 428 different homes. These designs use only forty percent of the energy required of the typical American home built in the early 1980s. MCS houses, which utilized techniques such as solar heat pumps and mechanical ventilation systems, were then tested against four hundred existing homes.

Not only did this program finally quantify the benefits of better building practices, it also demonstrated how American government can help deliver a large-scale conservation program. Indeed, the MCS homes have been further used to test new windows, Japanese refrigerators, and indoor ventilation systems. At last,

America is poised to develop homes as honorable as those in Sweden.

In addition, the BPA began investigating a negative aspect of tighter homes: indoor air pollution. If pollutants already exist within your home, measures that reduce the amount of air exchange by thirty percent can, in some instances, result in a corresponding increase in indoor air pollutants. The substances in question are suspected carcinogens, especially formaldehyde, benzene, toluene, and known household dangers such as mercury in split batteries, lead in paints, and even the fumes from car gas in basement garages.

Indoor Health Risks

Taxpayers may find it ironic that they have been billed more than $100 billion to underwrite government programs to reduce outdoor levels of perilous carbon monoxide and nitrogen dioxide gases when exposure to these gases is most likely to be found in the home. While the image of the oil refinery—its smell and smoke—is often disturbing, an 1980 EPA study in Bayonne, New Jersey, the site of a petrochemical plant, showed that the presence of eleven toxic chemicals was two to five times, and in one case seventy times, stronger indoors than out. You could inhale both carbon monoxide and nitrogen dioxide in the basement near your furnace, in the kitchen by your gas stove, or by the fireplace in your living room.[4]

Then there is radioactive radon gas. Radon is a natural gas that seeps from soil into homes through cracks in foundations. You can't smell or see it, and it occurs naturally, killing five thousand to twenty thousand people a year. Recent EPA studies show that one out of three homes tested exceeded the maximum recommended concentrations, and between one and two percent had levels that required immediate action.

Many toxins found in homes occur naturally, but their most insidious health effects are the result of man-made applications. One example is formaldehyde, which affects between 5 million and 20 million people every day, according to Professor Thad Godish at Ball State University. Symptoms include memory loss, depression, and gynecological problems. Formaldehyde is in your countertops, deodorants, and plywood, among other places. According to Commerce Department statistics, products containing formaldehyde constitute more than twenty percent of our nation's gross national product.

Many activities we participate in on a daily basis can be harmful to your health. Biochemist Bruce Ames of the University of California–Berkeley, a leader in risk-assessment research who designed the now-common Ames test for carcinogens, argues that cooking food generates more mutagens and carcinogens each day than one inhales from Los Angeles smog. Ames's recent work has spawned significant controversy by claiming that extrapolating cancer tests from animals to humans may not be valid. He has also claimed that natural cancer-causing elements in food, such as aflatoxins in peanut butter, are often more dangerous to one's health than drinking tainted drinking water supplies. "The idea that nature is benign and that evolution has allowed us to cope perfectly with toxic chemicals in the natural world is not compelling," summarizes Ames. His critique will not sit well with most of those engaged in the environmental masquerade, in spite of his work's relevance.

Regardless of Ames's assertions, a variety of ills associated with man-made toxins, now referred to as the multiple chemical sensitivities (MCS) syndrome, may prove to be a significant twenty-first-century disease. According to estimates by the National Academy of Sciences, about fifteen percent of the total population may already be affected with MCS. Our use of a variety of household products has had a devastating impact on a growing number of lives. Dana Miller, for instance, chose to live in a tent along unsprayed lands near Texas's Blanco River because of violent reactions to a common household insecticide. After spending four years and $400,000 in medical bills to recover, she has abandoned Harvard Law School and ekes out an existence to escape MCS. She represents a new kind of American—the industrialized homeless.[5]

Workplaces are also common sites for MCS victims. Researchers now single out dry-cleaning, chemical, plastics, textiles, painting, metalwork, wood-processing, printing and dye plants, and hospitals, as well as gas stations and laboratories. Think of how common these sites are in your neighborhoods, from suburban Long Island to the ghettos of Los Angeles and Chicago. Individual susceptibility to chemicals varies, but it appears that women are particularly vulnerable, comprising eighty percent of documented hypersensitive cases so far.

These toxins also affect children. The nation's first study on reproductive hazards in the workplace was undertaken by the Women's Health Unit of the Massachusetts Department of Public Health and the University of Massachusetts Medical Center.[6] Released in November 1988, the report dramatizes how complacent many employers are.

The study discovered that fifty-four percent of the 105 companies using chemicals known to be dangerous to pregnant mothers lacked any reproductive-hazards guidelines. Of the total sample surveyed—198 companies—fifty-three percent reported using one of the four known toxins most dangerous to newborns. Yet only forty percent of the firms who used these known dangers acknowledged that they posed harm to childbearing women.

For children, one of the most common household hazards is peeling lead-based paints. Preschool children love to stick things in their mouths, and absorption of lead is particularly dangerous when it is ingested alone. The ingestion has caused cognitive and neurobehavioral dysfunctions. Recent epidemiological studies show that an estimated 675,000 children between the ages of six months and five years have lead poisoning—because close to half of the nation's housing stock is primed with these toxic paints.

Reoccupying Your Home

Whether in the workplace or the home, we must reduce levels of harmful substances. One simple way to reduce formaldehyde levels fifty percent is to cool your house by ten degrees. This both saves energy and reduces the volatility of this domestic hazard.

Another useful tool to reduce existing levels of formaldehyde, and of many other harmful pollutants as well, is houseplants. NASA research into the use of plants to purify the air in future manned space missions is now proving to have applications in the home. The spider plant, as well as the peace lily, golden pathos, and Chinese evergreen have proven to be especially effective filters for benzene, carbon monoxide, carbon dioxide, and other common household chemicals. Dr. Bill Wolverton, a NASA research scientist, estimates that as few as fifteen houseplants may significantly clean the air in the average home. The Foliage for Clean Air Council, a Virginia-based consortium of private entrepreneurs, also promotes the use of houseplants combined with charcoal filtering systems to absorb troublesome pollutants such as cigarette smoke and dust particles.

Another answer is substitute products. Researchers at the University of Wisconsin at Madison have discovered a way to convert formerly discarded cheese whey from America's dairyland into a formaldehyde-free adhesive to make particle board, as well as a new insulating foam that is cheaper to fireproof than conventional polyurethane foams.

These are just a few examples. Consumers need more information about these alternatives, and industry must respond by transforming laboratory promises into commercial products.[7] America has already taken steps to replace unsafe products, such as polychlorinated biphenyls (PCBs) and the insecticide DDT.

Given that the world uses more than seventy thousand chemicals every day, sorting out which ones are safe is no small job. Nonetheless, the lack of information on the properties of the vast majority of these chemicals is hardly reassuring to families concerned about their children's health. The National Research Council estimates that seventy-nine percent of the close to fifty thousand chemicals yet to be analyzed by the Environmental Protection Agency have, to date, no established safety limits. The growing number of incidents of known environmental damage that has resulted from our blindly putting volatile chemicals into our homes has become too great to ignore.

Fortunately, a "soft chemistry" movement now under way in Europe helps to point out some indoor solutions. Both the Social Democratic Party and the Christian Democratic Union of the Federal Republic of Germany favor the printing of an "environmental price" on products. This "price" would include an objective gauge of the toxic emissions released in the creation, use, and disposal of the product. Such a law, if implemented in the United States, could have a profound economic impact on firms who fail to consider the consumer's new concern for a clean home.

You can shape public policy on these matters, because your purchasing decisions are the equivalent of voting in an economic election. Businesses are aware of this power, and in response have developed new, nonpolluting, biodegradable diapers, one-hundred-percent recycled paper, and solar-powered batteries, wristwatches, and Walkmans. Substitutes for toxic products can be used, too, including nontoxic flea powder, plant insecticides, toilet cleaners, and laundry soap. Entire catalogues now feature these "real goods."

It should not be forgotten that many products in your home may actively threaten our upper atmosphere. Common household items such as aerosol deodorants, shaving creams, and hair sprays, and that ever-comforting air conditioner, have contributed close to half of the culprits (CFCs) that now help punch holes in the ozone, allowing more of the sun's damaging ultraviolet radiation through.[8] Medical authorities report a thirty-percent increase in skin cancer over the course of the last decade, a direct result of consumer choices we have previously made.

The dawning of a new era may be upon us, however. In spring 1989, some eighty nations recognized that the well-publicized Montreal Protocol of 1987 was already out of date and that a larger worldwide effort was needed. Through a series of international conferences, it was established that substitutes already exist for CFCs in many of their past uses. For instance, a nontoxic natural product derived from orange peels can replace the freon formally used to degrease the solvents used in manufacturing computer chips and circuit boards. McDonald's replaced Styrofoam packaging with a product manufactured with a different CFC that breaks down in the lower atmosphere and therefore does not disrupt the ozone layer. The speed of this second wave of changes is encouraging.

Efforts to reverse the tide of environmentally unsound economics are not limited to stopping mistakes. Establishing new markets is also needed. Anthropologist-turned-entrepreneur Jason Clay of

Boston is now marketing a whole range of products derived from the fast-disappearing Amazon jungles, including a whole line of ice creams produced by Vermont-based Ben and Jerry's. Flavors such as "Rain Forest Crunch," as well as sherbets that will be available on a rotating basis according to when jungle fruits are in season, are already on the shelves. Future endeavors include rain forest foods, as well as health and beauty aids. Even a condom made from natural rubber with the logo "Protect Yourself and Protect the Rain Forest" is in the works.

Clay, a graduate of Harvard and the London School of Economics, says the idea behind these ventures "is to stop saying no to everything in the Amazon, and start offering a positive alternative to people who need to make a living there." He added that studies show that a living forest produces more wealth than one that is raped for inappropriate farming or ranching schemes. "Now it's time to start testing that claim in the marketplace." Products will be purchased from cooperatives run by traditional rain forest Indians and rubber tappers. Clay expects business to reach $50 million within five years.

Your Car

Your car is the single largest cause for most serious air pollutants. Over one hundred million Americans now live in urban areas with ambient ozone levels in excess of National Ambient Air Quality Standards (NAAQS), largely because of exhaust from ever-increasing numbers of cars.

Our attachment to cars,[9] observes historian Martin Melosi, helped precipitate the Great Depression. The market for autos was saturated in such a short time period that the sharp drop-off in manufacturing caused a major decline in the economy at large. This role cars can play was reasserted in the 1970s. Melosi notes that it was "urban growth and rural penetration stimulated by the automobile which brought 'the machine in the garden,' reduced places of natural beauty, and broke rural seclusion." The car is simply our most destructive everyday technology. By 1924, the car already was causing 700,000 injuries and $1 billion in property damage annually.

Despite the danger—or maybe because of the thrill—cars have long been a symbol of independence for Americans. The epitome of this attitude is found in California, particularly on the Los Angeles freeways. Today Los Angeles is paying the price for this testament to upward mobility with smog that usually obscures whole snow-capped mountain ranges from view.

Radical changes are in store. According to South Coast Air Quality Management District plans, all L.A. cars will need to run on clean fuels such as electricity or solar cells twenty years from now. Already, nine thousand L.A.–based companies are drawing up ride-sharing programs for use in 1990. Major employers such as Hughes Aircraft, Litton Industries, and Northrup also have developed special programs to reduce traffic congestion, including cash payments for carpoolers. There is no other route remaining.

Lifestyle changes will be dramatic. Backyard barbecues will have to be limited, as will pleasure trips. Hair sprays and wood solvents will be banned or reformulated. Other changes will include the increased use of telecommuting, whereby you can stay at home to work by use of computers and other telecommunications

PUT THE SQUEEZE ON GASOLINE

Accelerate Your Vehicle Slowly

Accelerate gently except when entering high-speed traffic lanes or when passing. Rapid acceleration can increase fuel consumption by 2 miles per gallon in city traffic.

Air Conditioning Equipment

When in use, this equipment reduces fuel economy by as much as 2.5 miles per gallon.

Don't Carry Unnecessary Weight

For every additional 100 pounds, gas consumption can increase as much as 0.2 miles per gallon.

Get a Tune-up

Keep your car engine tuned according to the specifications given in your owner's manual. Every 10,000 miles, a major tune-up should be done. A tune-up can increase performance 3 percent.

Check Tire Pressure at Least Once a Month

Underinflated tires can decrease fuel economy by as much as 1 mile per gallon for every pound the tire is underinflated. Visual checks cannot determine underinflation until the tire is about 25 percent underinflated.

Source: Compiled from New York State Energy Office, Energy Hotline, and article for New York State Energy Office newsletter by Mary Barrett.

equipment. Since California has a disproportionate share of information workers—estimated to reach seventy percent of the working population by the year 2000—the California Energy Commission estimates that telecommuting could reduce current annual California gas consumption by over seven percent by the turn of the century.

New kinds of cars will play an important role.[10] At present, the state of California has worked out arrangements with Ford and General Motors to produce 2,200 flexible-fuel cars by 1993: cars that can run on gasoline, methanol, or ethanol, the latter two allegedly being the cleaner-burning fuels of the future. The California Energy Commission has arranged for the Atlantic Richfield Company and Chevron to market methanol fuel at some fifty filling stations.

Air-quality problems are hardly limited to urban Los Angeles and California. Along the Appalachian mountain chain, the acidity of cloud moisture often equals that of lemon juice. Agricultural losses attributed to nationwide air pollution, fueled increasingly by the car, have been estimated at approximately $5 billion annually since 1980.[11]

Increasing the fuel efficiency of today's gasoline-powered cars is the most important next step in the search for environmental excellence.[12] A complacent Detroit in the late 1980s had allowed, for the first time in fourteen years, American cars to be less efficient than previous generations. Hopefully, America's Big Three—General Motors, Ford, and Chrysler—will not forget the lessons of the 1970s, when the industry refused to adapt to changing consumer preferences and the reality that gas-guzzlers no longer made economic or environmental sense.[13]

There are signs that Detroit sees the writing on the wall. "If you want to participate in the shaping of public policy, you have to step forward and contribute to the solution or else you can't be a player. That wasn't the attitude that industry had in the 1970s," recalled Ford's vice president for environmental and safety engineering Helen Petrauskas.

One dramatic indication of things to come is the Methanol Marathon, a five-day, 1,100-mile road race between fourteen 1988 Chevrolet Corsicas souped up by students from different universities all across the country. The contest was sponsored by General Motors and allows mechanical engineering students to compete with their counterparts at rival universities to redesign the Corsica.

Even more forward-looking is GM's involvement with solar cars. The GM Sunraycer, a car twenty feet long, weighing only 547 pounds with driver, finished 620 miles ahead of the pack in the grueling 1987 World Solar Challenge. Since then the company has launched an educational program with more than 100,000 elementary and secondary schools participating. Colleges such as the California Institute of Technology have also used the Sunraycer as a case-study project.

To capitalize on America's competitive spirit, the GM Sunrayce USA, a south-to-north transcontinental race, was scheduled for July 1990. The product of cooperation between the federal Department of Energy, the Society of Automotive Engineers, Chevrolet, and universities throughout the land, the event promised to focus attention on the exciting possibilities of solar cars. It was to start from Florida's Disney World and end at GM's Technical Center in Warren, Michigan. "The race objective," according to GM president Robert Stempel, "is to stimulate interest in technical education and careers among students of all ages. In this sense, the event truly can be characterized as a race for our future."

Twenty-four-year-old entrepreneur James Worden is already chasing the solar-car dream. He expects to become the next Henry Ford. He and some of his colleagues at MIT want to mass produce solar cars. Worden made his first solar car while still in high school. Though his long-term goal is the development of "commuter cars," he and his fiancé are currently working on a sleek solar sports car that they anticipate will go sixty miles per hour, have a range of two hundred miles, and sell for $15,000.

Commentator Ellen Goodman has observed that the conventional car is the environmental equivalent of the cigarette, the equal-opportunity pollutant. Solar cars, on the other hand, represent a cleaner future when that sunny parking spot will take on a new appeal.

Your current car's use carries a significant environmental price tag. Every time you turn on that air conditioner, for instance, a little bit of ozone is being chipped away.[14]

One of the simplest ways to reduce the nasty effects your car has on local air quality is to drive less. Cities such as Phoenix, Arizona, already have programs where workers give up their cars one day a week. And in Sacramento, California, officials wrestling with increasing gridlock are considering the creation of so-called "pedestrian pockets." Half-mile-wide mini-cities of five thousand residents, each surrounded by a rural sea, these are the vision of Berkeley design professor Peter Calthorpe. The purpose of such pockets is not only to wean people away from their auto dependency, but to create a sense of place and community. Houses would be designed with front porches to encourage neighborly interaction; parking lots would be placed behind stores instead of in front, so that strolling shoppers don't feel intimidated.

These villages, linked by mass transit systems, would thoughtfully mix small businesses with residential homes. "The central focus is designing neighborhoods that don't force people to rely on the automobile for everything they want to do," observes Steve Sanders of the Environmental Council of Sacramento. The group's president, David Mogavero, adds: "We've got to start to develop land-use patterns where people can serve their needs by walking."

Your Backyard

There is a flip side to the realization that even your home may not be the safe haven you have so long thought it to be: Your yard is a wonderful part of the answer to worldwide environmental problems.[15]

We have all heard about the "not-in-my-backyard" syndrome, where you and others may have fought a waste-treatment facility near your neighborhood. What you may have overlooked is what we personally stash in our own backyards. A study conducted by the Division of Public Health at the University of Massachusetts at Amherst discovered that the most common pollutant we dump in our own backyards is automotive oil. On average, fourteen quarts were disposed of per household per year. Much of the rest of our country's oil is being deposited directly into public grounds, sewers, or local landfills.

This "out-of-sight, out-of-mind" attitude is a hard one to shake. Yet, if we expect manufacturers and government to stop polluting, we must also play our part.

The most insidious example of how people have polluted their own land comes from our family farms, where steady use of pesticides and fertilizers is now affecting private water wells. The EPA has discovered, for example, that in Minnesota, twenty-five percent of rural private wells contain nitrate levels that exceed safe standards for drinking water. In Iowa, the figure is forty percent; in Nebraska, seventy percent.

Even more dramatic evidence of self-poisoning comes from California's Central Valley, the most productive farm region in the world. In the small town of McFarland, children and young adults fear for their lives. Some have already died from cancer. Most feel the source of tragedy is contaminated drinking water, which is obtained from groundwater. DBCP, a chemical linked to birth defects, male sterility, and cancer, was found in wells throughout the valley. This should come as no real surprise. Californians have led the nation in pesticide use for years.

Toxic pesticide overuse is, of course, not limited to farms. A study by the National Academy of Sciences found that homeowners use from 5.3 to 10.6 pounds of pesticide per acre per year, actually many times the amount applied by farmers to corn and soybeans. Our incessant search for the perfect lawn has resulted in a misguided embrace of substances that could not only produce sterility and cancer in our children, but also creep into the food chain. Particularly nasty are organochlorines, which can accumulate in the food chain often to a million times normal levels.

We must recognize that simple things done in the yard—the use of nontoxic pest remedies, for example—play a vital role in the healing of environmental wounds. Small-scale acts can build geometrically. Giant vacuum cleaners now suck up bugs from acres of strawberry plants in Watsonville, California. This simple idea, discovered in someone's greenhouse, can now take care of pest worries without tainting drinking water. In this case, the use of the vacuum manages to suck up the harmful bugs on the top third of the plant, while leaving undisturbed the beneficial insects on the bottom third of the plants. Pesticides have never been able to do that.

In addition, the concept of introducing beneficial insects to maintain the health of your garden is now being expanded to include the use of certain bacteria to gobble up toxic waste. Some bugs actually survive only on toxic materials, so once they finish, they don't stick around. A recent EPA price estimate at a trouble spot in Crosby, Texas, showed that the use of microbes instead of incineration sliced cleanup costs by a third, saving $100 million.

Safer, Inc., a pioneer in natural pest controls, is also marketing Clandosian, a nontoxic, organic pesticide derived from shells of crabs and other shellfish. The waste products of one commerce group—the shellfish industry—are now used to kill the nematodes that often threaten California's tomato crops.

Like biological controls, trees are also marvelous tools. As we noted in the previous chapter, studies show that having three shade trees on the south and west sides of a house can lower air-conditioning bills by one-half. What's sensible for your yard also reduces carbon dioxide for the larger greenhouse. The American Forestry Association estimates that there are one hundred million spaces where trees could be planted around homes. If all of us planted trees, we would beautify our surroundings and our air quality would eventually improve greatly.

Environmental gains are now the business of young and old alike. Innovative government initiatives, such as New York State's Green Thumb program, are showing how a variety of tasks can be accomplished without huge government handouts for technology and big science. This program, funded by state monies, not only allows senior citizens an opportunity to make themselves useful by improving the grounds of parkways and government agencies, it also allows them to earn extra income that does not affect their Social Security. Saving the environment and enriching the lives of our nation's senior citizens, Green Thumb is the kind of multisolution program every region needs to enrich its future.

Technocracy is a cult. Technology will help revitalize America, but it isn't a god. The bigger answers revolve around common sense and your own backyard. This simple discovery will take Americans a long time to recognize, since the weight of our beliefs in technical complexity are so deep. This lasting faith in complexity was best displayed in the 1939 World's Fair in New York City.

The entire exhibit was constructed on top of a former swamp in Flushing, Queens—a swamp which F. Scott Fitzgerald aptly described as "a valley of ashes—a fantastic farm where ashes grow like wheat into ridges and hills and grotesque gardens bounded on one side by a small foul river." Years of abuse from the local railroads and construction contractors had rendered this urban axis a horrible place.

Transforming this pit into the fantastic 1,216.5-acre world's fair was the most ambitious land renovation project of its time. Conceived to bring Americans out of the dregs of the Depression, and designed to display the role technology would play in America's bright future, this world's fair was a public-relations masterpiece. A Rockwell Kent mural, for example, depicted how electrical research nurtured enlightenment. Others indicated why machines were like kings; a few suggested "Technos" was a god. The entire $160 million investment reflects, very well, a pattern of technical fantasies that has plagued our nation ever since.

Technology was equated with world peace in the 1939 World's Fair. The more we developed technologies—such as faster cars, electronic homes, and petro farms—the less war there would be because more and more people would have more and more technology. Planned traffic systems with seven hundred-mile-per-hour lanes were seen as guarantees of happiness, and energy supplies never appeared to be in question.

One of the most lavishly praised shows at the fair was the Petroleum Industry Exhibition, trumpeting the wonders of fossil fuels in puppet films such as "Pete-Roleum and His Cousins," laying the groundwork for our petrochemical treadmill. And a quick look down the Avenue of Patriots, where high-tech gadgets were displayed on pedestals, reveals how relentless our faith in technological fixes already had become. Familiar names such as General Electric, Westinghouse, and Du Pont—the names now connected with PCBs in the Hudson, cracks in Savannah reactors, and the costs of cleanup at Hanford—held magnificent shows then, each displaying an unbounded faith in technology and its triumph over nature.

World War II broke out. As the wondrously escapist world's fair continued to assert that peace rested in machines, millions were marching to war in Europe. When the fair closed prematurely on October 27, 1940, the nonprofit corporation that had been set up to run the events went bankrupt. Admissions had brought in only $48 million, whereas expenses had exceeded $67 million. The site underwent several conversions—among other things, it served as an ice-skating rink, and as temporary home to the United Nations—before it aptly became a park and zoo.

Today, fifty-one years after the 1939 World's Fair, technology still titillates us. For several decades, policies financing "mutual assured destruction" predicated world peace on a similar set of beliefs: Only by the constant production of an excess of nuclear weapons could we rest assured that technology might save the day. Some say the pattern is only intensifying, as powerful interests flirt with the notion that the changes in eastern Europe are only transient.

We say that most no longer want these dream machines. Most people want clean air, safe water supplies, places to rest and grow free from toxic materials—even if it means paying a price. Americans, and the rest of the world, are now ready for fresh policies that enlist citizens working through their own backyards.

Some twenty years ago, the American environmental movement was conceived on Earth Day—April 21, 1970. An estimated 20 million people took part in this moving recognition of the earth as a special sanctuary. This demonstration led to the creation of the EPA, our first environmental laws, and a cadre of environmental groups.

We are now witnessing the second wave of environmentalism. The National Audubon Society doubled its budget in 1989 and the Wilderness Society doubled its membership—all within a one-year period. We stand on the threshold of a new era of environmental awareness spreading to the corporate community and to individual citizens of all walks of life.

The twentieth anniversary of Earth Day 1990 was a significant milestone by which we measure how far we've come. The audiences were huge, and diverse, and responsive. While the power of protest and rallies still plays an important role today, the growth in environmental management and citizen participation is now making its mark in quieter, yet often more powerful ways. Tens of millions of Americans are growing or buying organic produce, recycling aluminum and glass, insulating their homes, and driving smaller cars.

The recognition that each person's backyard is everybody's backyard is underscored by the dramatic support offered by the Soviet Union, a Communist superpower that has often lagged behind the United States in addressing environmental issues. As Soviet Foreign Minister Edvard Shevardnadze said in an August 1989 address to the United Nations:

> The biosphere recognizes no division into blocs, alliances or systems. All share the same climatic system, and no one is in a position to build his own isolated and independent line of defense. All of us—and I emphasize this—all of us need an international program to manage the risks involved in economic activities and to shift to alternative technologies that spare both man and nature.

The world now needs an international "Green Cross," a system of transnational organizations like the Red Cross which cuts across institutional bias and drives the great environmental changes needed. Moreover, in addition to these larger changes in corporate structure and national behavior, it is each one of us, enlisting support on a local front, who helps make the difference.

Part Three

Future Solutions

Chapter 5

Industry and the Environment: Creating Affordable Beliefs

What defense has been to the world leaders for the past 40 years, the environment will be for the next 40: an attractive exercise in national self-restraint.

—THE ECONOMIST

Global warming. Hanford. *Valdez.*

As we enter the last decade of the twentieth century, are Americans prepared to pay the sizable environmental costs that lie ahead?

If 1989 is any indication, our budget chieftains believe in the wrong answers. While $6 trillion was afforded Star Wars, a blue-sky aspiration that many now consider more dream than reality, only $500 million was earmarked for energy research and development. What's worse, over ninety percent of these energy dollars were funneled into old options, financing massive clean-coal and enhanced oil-recovery efforts. Energy efficiency, the most utilitarian investment and the logical first step in any industrial revitalization, accounted for about five percent of the total energy budget.

How long can we afford such disproportionate investments? If America is to move beyond environmental gridlock in the next decades, three dangerously entrenched fallacies must first be overcome. These are:

- *Things do not change rapidly.* This notion, more than any other attitude, has hindered the search for environmental excellence over the last forty years. Endless litigation over flawed regulations, which even when improved can still be circumvented, is clearly not the most practical way to pursue environmental excellence. Nations can speed up environmental progress tremendously by harnessing market forces and through the use of private capital.

• *Government and industry are natural enemies when it comes to the environment.* This peculiar cultural quirk makes Americans spend a great deal of energy spinning their wheels. We have to stop pretending that the best deal in business is to scam government and vice versa. Instead we need to realize that big problems require joint ventures. Public-private partnerships in Japan and Europe offer useful examples, some worthy of adaptation.

• *The economy and the environment are in direct and vicious conflict.* Impaired economic thinking has for too long short-changed the earth. To believe we can have a sound economy only by incurring severe environmental costs is unsophisticated, but this false dualism is deeply ingrained in American institutions. New challenges, however, such as the need to compete with more efficient foreign manufacturing capacity, demonstrate that the answers to economic and environmental problems are often the same.

Moving beyond these misconceptions will not be easy; an illusion of certainty surrounds these three sticking points. But significant change is now occurring, pointing to a more affordable approach to economics and the environment.

One early example lies on an abandoned industrial site on the outskirts of Davis, California, and is known in the energy trade as PVUSA. PVUSA, which stands for Photovoltaics for Utility Scale Applications, is a world-class "solar supermarket" where inventive arrays of solar cells are being tested to find out which approaches will be the most competitive in tomorrow's world market. Photovoltaics (PVs), a solar technology that utilizes semiconductors to generate electricity, is but one of the many new energy technologies that combine the world's new environmental standards with the practical needs of industry.[1]

While U.S. researchers remain world leaders in defense, medicine, and agriculture, West Germany and Japan are already selling PV panels for American rooftops. The challenge ahead became painfully clear when America's brightest light in the PV arena— ARCO Solar—was purchased in 1989 by Siemens AG of West Germany. Though the Germans receive only half the insolation (a measurement of the incoming solar radiation that makes it possible to produce electricity) that the United States does, the astute German government will be spending $58 million, in contrast to our $36 million, in fiscal year 1990 for the development of this answer to global warming and acid rain. They simply view solar energy in the right light—as a more affordable and benign kind of energy, quite likely to take off in the next century as oil did in the previous one.

ARCO Solar, though well respected for its products, had difficulty justifying waiting out the development period. In contrast, Siemens is taking a long-term view. "We measure all of our performance and do all of our planning in a five-year time frame," one executive was quoted in the *Energy Daily*. "I couldn't imagine having to worry so much about quarterly financial results the way U.S. executives do."

A few forward-looking U.S. utility executives, manufacturers, and government officials, however, understand America's need to coordinate its energy expertise more effectively to prepare for the future; hence, PVUSA. The research effort is a joint venture between the California Energy Commission, the federal Department of Energy, Pacific Gas & Electric (the largest investor-owned utility in the world), and other utilities from across the country. Eventually between fifteen and thirty competing 20-kilowatt arrays will be plugged into a computer analysis system that will provide the information base for America's mission to secure markets for tomorrow's clean-energy technologies. The project is slated to cost only $40 million, a tiny blip compared to the towering expenditures on fossil-fuel and nuclear research. Utilities in climates as vastly different as Virginia, New York, and Hawaii are interested in PVUSA, demonstrating its wide range of regional applications.

Photovoltaics reduce our dependence on fossil fuels. In addition, obtaining the permits to operate a small-scale photovoltaic plant can take six months. The typical permit process for a fossil-fuel site can last up to six years. The principal roadblock to widespread acceptance of photovoltaics has been cost, storage of power, and finding locations with enough consistent sunshine.

All of these roadblocks are now being broken. Pacific Gas & Electric has already carried out over four hundred cost-effective installations of photovoltaics, using them in such diverse applications as cloud seeders and aircraft warning beacons.

The work of PVUSA displays the value of American efforts to assemble world-class researchers for results outside of defense, medicine, or agriculture. It also represents an important counterpart to Japan's Rokko Island, a location where one hundred different 2-kilowatt solar systems, designed by approximately a half dozen Japanese manufacturers, are lined up side by side for vigorous head-to-head competition to determine which photovoltaic product Japan will use to try to dominate the world market. We may be witnessing a major energy revolution in the 1990s; if American manufacturers don't want to see the photovoltaic market go the route of cars, electronics, and other current imported technologies, then R&D efforts such as PVUSA need to be expanded to include the whole range of alternative energy paths.

But America, despite the isolated efforts of facilities like PVUSA, has been moving in the opposite direction. For fiscal year 1990, the federal Office of Management and Budget recommended a thirty-percent cut in photovoltaic research funding, along with approximately twenty-percent cuts in solar-thermal and solar-buildings research. These proposed cuts were preceded by an eighty-percent reduction in all solar program funding in a seven-year period beginning in 1981.[2]

In contrast, the Japanese have steadily supported photovoltaics over the past ten years. They surpassed the U.S. in photovoltaic funding levels in the late 1980s, investing $48 million in 1988. In a tale that is becoming all too familiar to American manufacturers, the Japanese and other competitors are now on the brink of commercializing photovoltaics, a technology which the United States pioneered and began promoting over a decade ago.

We are primed to lose in the race for renewables. American development of clean sources of power, such as photovoltaics, peaked in 1989 and will fall off sharply throughout the first half of the 1990s. As Susan Williams, an analyst with the Investor Responsibility Research Center, observes: "It's an irony that just as policymakers and the general public are latching onto the benefits of renewables, we're poised for a big decline." The United States once had eighty percent of the world's photovoltaic market. Today we have less than half. The budget cuts during the Reagan years are having a direct and vicious effect.

Given the environmental and economic dilemmas ahead, we can no longer afford to let our competitors pass us by. Energy is a key link in securing environmental excellence. If we ignore this basic tenet, America once again will be dependent upon foreign countries for the fuels of tomorrow.

The Real Japanese Threat

In recent decades the Japanese have demonstrated a keen understanding of the pace and requirements of affordable industrial research and development. History attests to their success. Within forty years, they have risen from the ashes of atomic holocaust to become the leading creditor nation on the planet. Japan's success can be directly attributed to its innovative research approaches to complex resource problems and its uncanny ability to translate daring ideas into efficient commercial products. An array of research institutions, such as their new National Institute of Resources, works directly with government and business and is designed to tackle the tough economic and environmental questions that darken the world's current industrial outlook.

Whereas Americans remain hobbled by fallacious beliefs about the interplay of energy, the environment, and the economy, Japan has mastered the art of balancing "the three E's." For example, the National Institute of Resources is driven by three alternative principles, each of which challenges American beliefs, and fuels a more coherent kind of industrial research and development. First, all funded research responds to existing technological and scientific needs: the emphasis is on improvements, enhancements, and efficiency, not the splash of a near-term breakthrough. Second, the institute works to help these upgrades penetrate the market in an accelerated fashion. Finally, development tasks are conceived from a global perspective; the work is designed to apply to a pool of consumers much larger than any narrow domestic market.

Many of the advantages Japan now enjoys over the United States can be traced back to strong cultural and geographical roots. While Americans have viewed their country as the land of superabundance, the Japanese have taken a more pragmatic approach to their limited resources: waste not, want not. Japan has had to struggle to overcome its natural-resource handicaps, but its vigorous efforts have enabled the nation to form a disciplined industrial complex acutely aware of the long term. The Japanese are unexcelled in industrial research and innovation, and in their timely quest for efficiency.[3]

Slightly smaller than the state of California, Japan imports over ninety-five percent of its iron, tin, and copper, as well as most of its lead and zinc. Japan is also the world's largest importer of coal, natural gas, and oil. It provides only eight percent of its own natural gas and nineteen percent of its coal requirements. Far more the fossil-fuel addict than the States, it has had to achieve maximum efficiency as early as technically possible.

No one doubts that these handicaps have played a major role in prompting the Japanese to be so frugal.

One startling statistic from Daniel J. Boorstin's recent book *Yen!* epitomizes the success of the Japanese model of innovation. The world's largest ten banks are all Japanese, despite the fact that thirty years ago not one bank from Japan ranked in the top fifty. The Japanese now dominate the world's financial empire. But even more important than the long list of Japanese conquests in the international marketplace is its role in stimulating more adept applications for industrial needs in areas where their American counterparts have abandoned ship. As American venture capitalists shirk their responsibilities in more efficient high technology, the Japanese have eagerly filled the void. One in every fifteen new dollars invested in new, high-tech companies worldwide now comes from Japanese sources.

McGraw-Hill's *Independent Power Report* predicted that $42 billion will be invested in U.S. independent power projects between 1989 and 1995. According to *The American Banker*, foreign banks, including Japan's Fuji Bank, Sumitomo, and Nippon

Credit Bank of Japan, now finance half the $5 billion a year lent to such U.S. energy projects. This competition has slashed fees and interest rates for financing, stimulating more U.S. projects but discouraging domestic investments from gun-shy American bankers.

The Normura Research Institute predicts that one day Tokyo will surpass New York as the financial center of the world. "We must start preparing the infrastructure now. We must be able to lead history, rather than try to catch up to it," is the way a Normura spokesman summarized the Japanese ambition. This attention to long-term commitments and sustained progress stands in stark contrast to contemporary America's ways. According to the National Science Foundation, real U.S. government support for nondefense R&D declined by seventeen percent between 1980 and 1983, while support for basic research declined by 1.7 percent. Instead of developing a comprehensive long-term policy framework designed to revitalize American industries while addressing energy and environmental concerns, we, in the words of New York Senator Daniel Patrick Moynihan, "borrowed a trillion dollars from the Japanese and threw a party."

Japan and America's divergent paths have, to the detriment of our economy, complemented one another in a perverse way. However, Berkeley political scientist John Zysman cautions that a United States–Japan "divorce" could occur by the year 2000.

Responding to the Threat

The debate over how to enable America to compete has, until now, hardly drawn any firm conclusions. *Industrial policy* has become a buzzword. Many, such as the well-known analysts Ira Magaziner and Robert Reich, have argued that government should provide assistance to ailing or emerging U.S. industries. The drawback of such an approach is that too much government involvement could distract businesses, particularly if environmental safeguards are sacrificed, while distorting the marketplace with protectionist subsidy wars.

If some elements of such an approach were to be indeed institutionalized, recommends Robert Lawrence of the Brookings Institute, author of *Can America Compete?*,[4] government assistance programs should focus on: permanent efficiency trends, not fad industries; innovations that have the potential to improve resource allocation; and environmentally sound industrial practices that improve America's competitive edge. These principles, which fly in the face of the fallacies dominating most American economic planning, are far more lasting than the "clear and present" political needs of a specific company or organized industry. Renewable-energy research and development, as well as waste-reduction techniques, would give us things to fight for rather than against.

America's research and technological successes in the fields of defense, agriculture, and medicine, as Don Kash points out in his book *Perpetual Innovations,*[5] were assisted by an urgency brought about by the crisis of World War II. Since then, a large organizational complex has evolved, composed of government agencies, contractors, and universities, that requires "continuous innovation" in order to prosper. This American model established an aggressive working partnership between researchers, industry, and government where financial risks attending technical failure were softened, allowing for creative experimentation.

In contrast, the Japanese history of government-supported technological innovation has been driven by commercial concerns focused on international cost-competitiveness and a spiral of incremental innovations that have shortened the innovation-to-obsolescence cycles for many consumer products. Many of us forget that Japanese transistor radios used to be the laughingstock of the trade in the sixties. By the seventies, Japanese products such as Sony televisions were the state of the art. In the eighties, the ever-shortening cycles of innovation have resulted in products of superior performance, higher quality, and lowest cost. Indeed, by October 1984, Japan was making over 2.6 million VCRs each month, while U.S. output had declined to zero.

The Japanese government, perceiving the need for radical innovations in industrial efficiency, has organized a number of unique nonprofit research projects for the purpose of bringing leading companies together to work on common projects of high national priority—avoiding wasteful duplication, pooling finite resources, and achieving research economies of scale. Though these research centers are nonprofit, their goal is to create commercial products. This kind of coordination is unheard of in America; perhaps this is one reason why our commercialization of technical breakthroughs is so much slower than Japan's and why our basic manufacturing processes are so often obsolete.

Though companies provide the bulk of R&D monies in Japan (seventy-three percent), the government identifies key "precompetitive research areas" for government guidance and assistance, playing a role akin to our Department of Defense's linking of institutions for weapons development. Indeed, the Japanese have posed for the United States commercial sector the same kind of challenge that we have posed for the Soviets in the military sector. The most effective way for the United States to answer this Japanese challenge will be to develop new international markets in energy products and environmental technologies.

The United States' current R&D contract system is based on three consistent goals: a push for state-of-the-art expertise and specialization; the development of funding mechanisms to enable diverse organizations with different motives to pursue joint objectives; and the translation of this cooperation into a synergistic routine whereby innovations represent more than the sum of their parts, stimulating spinoffs and further social benefits. This contract structure, notes Kash, has been, for the most part, a success story. Until now, however, the nation has never focused this vast R&D arsenal on environmental concerns and benign energy needs, and instead has been preoccupied with short-term production goals. It is time to rework the American model and apply a new set of incentives to promote popular environmental reforms.

For too long, America's industrial leaders have been fostering the idea that economics and the environment are in direct and vicious conflict. Some business executives continue to complain that increased environmental safeguards will drive their factories to foreign shores and make America into a nation of ghost towns. A study conducted by H. Jeffrey Leonard of the Conservation Foundation dispels many of these myths.[6] The report documents the fact that no large-scale exodus has occurred due to regulatory burdens, and concludes that a relaxation of regulatory standards would not restore U.S. competitiveness, but rather "would remove an important incentive for technological progress, as well as increase worker- and public health-hazards."

In reality, environmental goals—the striving for clean land, air, water and energy—have now become economic and national security goals. America's thirty thousand Love Canals, with their $50 billion cleanup bill, the $200 billion crash program to clean up our weapons complex, and the need to combat global warming all reveal the same recurring lesson. If the full costs of polluting had been factored in up front since World War II, America would not be facing these world-scale cleanup challenges, since it would have made good business sense to reduce waste, save materials, and conserve energy from the outset.

For the last thirty years, the dumping of toxic debris has burdened society with unpaid bills. Most companies have looked at pollution as something that comes out of a pipe somewhere, and has to be treated somehow. Even when treatment units work properly, they usually transfer the problem from the water to the air or vice versa. Lax regulatory standards have resulted in some reduction of conspicuous pollutants, such as oxygen-robbing sewage dumped into rivers, but have ignored more difficult and serious problems, such as the seeping of heavy metals into the ground. Reliable enforcement of existing controls has proven to be elusive because of a lack of government resources, heavy paperwork burdens, and the existence of too many loopholes in the laws.

There are, however, success stories that prove that environmentally sound practices make economic sense. The 3M Company, the acknowledged dean in waste reduction, has cut its hazardous-waste generation for all plants almost in half over the past decade. As of March 1988, the firm's "Pollution Prevention Pays" program saved $420 million, and prevented the annual discharge of 1.6 billion tons of wastewater, 120,000 tons of air pollutants, 14,000 tons of water pollutants, and 313,000 tons of sludge and solid waste. The firm is setting goals on reducing its current waste streams by another thirty percent between 1990 and 1995.

The Dow Chemical Company is following 3M's lead. In 1986, the firm initiated its "Waste Reduction Always Pays" program.

Ryan Delcambre, the manager at Dow who initiated these waste-reduction efforts, now boasts that "there's money to be made in waste reduction," pointing out that Dow's Louisiana division has saved $5.2 million and reduced its waste by 250 million pounds since 1984. By 1989, other Dow projects were estimated to have reaped $6 million just in raw-materials savings.

Such efforts by private industry are welcome—but government needs to help pave the road to greater efficiency. By providing a blueprint for widespread reforms in all U.S. industries, the nation would strike a more affordable bargain with the future, and at last directly address in business terms the increasing environmental costs and liabilities of the old ways of managing.

One promising move in the right direction is *Project 88: Harnessing Market Forces to Protect Our Environment*,[7] which was sponsored by Democratic Senators Tim Wirth of Colorado and John Heinz of Pennsylvania. This report's critical contribution to the political dialogue is its fresh look at how we as a nation can advance beyond the pitfalls of the three false policy assumptions mentioned earlier. The report attempts to answer this fundamental question: How can we ensure that investment in environmental protection is cost-effective, so that we can enhance our international competitive strength while we build a better environment? Perhaps the political arena, with its strong taste for compromise, can strike the policy balance needed.

As this report notes, "Utilizing market forces and economic common sense to achieve environmental goals entails removing market barriers and governmental subsidies which promote economically inefficient and environmentally unsound practices." An incentive-based approach will reap another important benefit: it will make environmental choices more understandable to business and thus quicken the pace of progress.

The good news is that *Project 88* represents a new and forceful political alliance and an agenda that concisely sums up many of the goals we term "affordable beliefs." Politicians voting with *Project 88* goals in mind will answer the most disturbing questions about the greenhouse effect and the need to balance energy and environmental concerns. Here is a sampling of goals:

- To fund research on causes and consequences of, and on adaptation and prevention strategies for, the greenhouse effect.
- To promote energy efficiency and development of alternative fuels.
- To offset new sources and set up international trading of greenhouse gases.
- To prevent deforestation through debt-forest swaps.
- To improve population policies.
- To strengthen motor-vehicle fuel-efficiency standards.
- To provide incentives for efficient vehicles and alternative fuels.
- To increase energy efficiency through comprehensive least-cost bidding at electrical utilities.
- To fund research on alternatives to fossil fuels.

Often these nine goals share the same political liabilities and results. To push for one often results in the others. That's what's so attractive to the politicians behind *Project 88*: it adds up, and each step they take echoes throughout the corridors of Congress. The following quote from the report recapitulates the challenge before us: "If Theodore Roosevelt's conservation ethic at the beginning of this century represented the first important era of environmental concern in the United States, then the decade of important new laws and regulations following Earth Day was the second era. Our challenge now is to move aggressively into a third era—a period when practical and economically sensible policies will provide more effective and efficient management of natural resources and protection of the environment."

The political pursuit of more efficient windows, turbines, and cars represents an important force for the revitalization of American industry, but there are other, less political, avenues as well. The information age is upon us, and—despite the difficulty of diffusing the knowledge of environmental-excellence successes throughout the marketplace—the power of information can aid pivotal investments. By directing the growing ranks of socially conscious investors, the recently formulated "Valdez Principles," constitute a significant redirection.

These investor guidelines draw their inspiration from the Sullivan Principles, a set of self-imposed investment principles that spotlighted companies' ties to apartheid in South Africa. Though the specifics of an environmental-investment report card still need to be fine-tuned, the establishment of such a rating system is inevitable in today's information age. Annual environmental review audits will steer investment dollars in the future, rewarding those firms that wisely manage their operations, and punishing those who take unwise environmental risks. A favorable review for a given company will generate goodwill among consumers and shareholders; therefore, adhering to the Valdez Principles will give companies a competitive edge.

Half a Pair of Scissors

The greatest sin associated with our preoccupation with fossil fuels is that we are losing sixty to eighty percent of their potential energy due to inefficient combustion processes that create pollution instead of energy. Cogeneration—a term originally coined in the 1880s that refers to the generation of two types of energy from one fuel source—was once the norm in this country. With the discovery of abundant oil, however, industry began to pay less attention to efficiency. Of the 16 million barrels of oil this thirsty nation consumes every day, more than eighty-five percent is used in monogeneration systems functioning at twenty- to forty-percent efficiency.

America's present search for environmental excellence is reminiscent of its 1970s response to the energy crisis: an attempt to recapture the ingenuity that marked our early industrialization. As a nation we were forced to acknowledge that reducing our dependence on imported oil was only half of a solution. The other, more difficult half involved the reestablishment of energy-conserving technologies such as cogeneration.[8] Similarly, today Americans must restructure our response to the environmental challenge. We must mobilize a probusiness response that reduces and treats the nation's toxic waste load at its source, using the marketplace to stimulate needed reforms.

So far, we have only been using one-half of the scissors to cut out the problem: regulations. Though these well-intentioned laws, such as the Superfund cleanup program and the Clean Air Act, have forced American industry to pay attention to environmental issues, too often their purpose has been circumvented. The other half of the scissors is business-development guidance and assistance that fosters environmental excellence.

No one—except free-market ideologues—would openly argue that regulations have not helped. They have brought environmental components into the everyday plans of American industry. Occasionally, however, a stray example of regulatory failure highlights the complexity of the task before us. In Ohio, for instance, the EPA's state plan for enforcing the Clean Air Act of 1970 ended up promoting further pollution, rather than preventing it.[9]

Coal-fired electric plants produce and emit sulfur dioxide into the atmosphere, which contributes to acid rain and can cause human health problems. One way to reduce these emissions is to burn low-sulfur coal. Because of transportation costs associated with importing supplies from Wyoming and Montana, however, low-sulfur coal is more expensive than high-sulfur coal for an Ohio utility. Other methods for reducing emissions include the "washing" of high-sulfur coal and the retrofitting of existing plants with scrubbers. These scrubbers, when they work, can remove over ninety percent of the unwanted emissions, but this approach is much more costly than using low-sulfur coal.

The most logical solution is to use low-sulfur Western coal, yet that choice was opposed by the United Mine Workers. They saw this regulatory battle as a bread-and-butter issue for miners in southeastern Ohio, and, working with environmentalists and Eastern coal interests, pushed for the most expensive solution—the installation of scrubbers.

The new regulations requiring scrubbers would only be imposed on new generating plants, however. Indeed, a new electric power plant built after 1979 is mandated to reduce sulfur-dioxide emissions per kilowatt-hour by eighty-four percent compared to a plant built in 1971. This discrepancy ultimately stymies the regulatory intent. A utility that is precluded from switching fuels typically postpones the construction of new plants and the associated scrubbing costs, and therefore continues to burn more polluting coal in old plants as long as possible.

Despite these drawbacks, the EPA was directed, in amendments to the Clean Air Act in 1977, to avoid economic disruption or regional unemployment in locations where pollution was being reduced. Ironically, after these amendments passed, Ohio utilities discovered that sources of low-sulfur coal in nearby Kentucky and West Virginia had become available because of the decline of the steel industries there. Yet another political battle erupted over the use of regional, not state, coal. In the end, Ohio utilities succeeded in convincing the EPA that it could continue to burn high-sulfur coal without scrubbers—because the utilities did not, by their own estimation, violate sulfur dioxide standards after all.[10]

The shortcomings exposed in the Ohio coal regulations show how urgently we need a comprehensive strategy to revitalize American industry without limiting special interests. One of the most coherent appraisals of the task before us is Robert G. Healy's *America's Industrial Future: An Environmental Perspective.*[11] Healy observes that technological change holds no guarantees for the environment. Furthermore, even when new environmentally benign processes are developed, it takes too long for these innovations to be adopted. "Government should therefore take more responsibility for promoting the introduction of low-pollution production methods in heavy industry," states Healy. He notes that the needed cooperation between government and private industry has been limited in the United States "by an ideological conviction that individual industrial firms should bear the entire responsibility for process innovation." Yet, he argues, by defining the issue of saving the environment as a public-sector problem, America should be able to rethink its biases.

Too often, the U.S. government is nowhere to be seen when it comes to developing stimulants for industry to operate efficiently. The results of this shortcoming are becoming increasingly evident. A study conducted by INFORM, an environmental research organization, disclosed that in a study sample of twenty-nine organic chemical plants, company waste-reduction incentives applied to less than one percent of wastes generated.[12]

The need for revitalization achieves an even greater significance when viewed from the perspective of international competition. According to Healy, American industries are falling behind because of a refusal to acknowledge a serious correlation between low profitability and a failure to invest in environmental upgrades. Firms doing poorly are typically those that disdain regulation, lobby for a relaxing of the standards, and are reluctant to invest in new energy-conservation equipment. The steel industry, for example, had an average 7.05-percent rate of profit throughout the 1970s and exemplifies this shortsightedness. On the other hand, the domestic paper industry, whose profitability ratio stands at 12.3 percent, has by and large upgraded its processes for modern environmental standards. These investments are paying off, as the paper industry uses fifteen percent less energy than it did in 1972, while it has increased production by over seventeen percent.

Too much of American industry, nevertheless, is characterized by old, inefficient processes. The electrolytic process by which we manufacture aluminum products has changed very little since 1886, the year the process was first introduced. Moreover, even when industrial innovations occur, it takes too long for widespread adoption of the innovations. Healy points out that one researcher who analyzed nine different petroleum refining processes discovered that it took an average of thirteen years for the new methods to become standard practice in the industry.

We have to change our machines, not just our laws.

A New Design Triangle

America's answer to the toxic waste dilemma hinges on a new industrial design triangle invented in Europe[13] and empowered by three unrelenting principles: conserve energy; save materials; and reduce waste. This design triangle meshes economic motives with environmental goals. It is a vital mix that breaks long-standing logjams between business, government, and concerned citizens.

Hundreds of industrial firms in Europe have implemented this conceptual triangle to reduce waste and improve profits.[14] One of the outstanding success stories from France is an innovative thermoreactor, a paint-drying technique developed by Sunkiss. This technique has been installed at metal-finishing operations for products ranging from small metal products to cars and locomotives. The use of this technique by France's Alstholm Atlantic on two of its metal-painting lines has yielded the following promising environmental and economic benefits:

- A ninety-nine-percent reduction in emissions of evaporated solvents, which are destroyed in the thermoreactor's catalytic heating/drying process.
- The elimination of the explosion risks usually associated with drying operations because of solvent fumes.
- A ninety-nine-percent reduction in drying time, which increases production and expedites automation on the painting lines.
- An eighty-percent savings in the energy requirements for the drying operations, which yields annual savings of 1.1 million francs.

The cost to Sunkiss for the purchase and installation of the thermoreactors was earned back in the form of savings in only two months.

Industry-government alliances here in the United States have already yielded some impressive results with very little startup capital. For instance, a partnership effort between the California Department of Health Services, entrepreneurs at Toxics Recovery Systems International, and the Anaheim-based AeroScientific Corporation, a manufacturer of printed-circuit boards, has resulted in an ingenious method for the treatment of heavy-metals waste.

This method transforms formerly discarded wastes from the production of circuit boards into solid metallic sheets which can be sold as scrap. The system can save a firm upward of $100,000 in legal bills alone, and can speed up business operations by eliminating the need for lengthy state or federal regulatory review. "The biggest advantage is that we'll be free from the enormous liability that companies face every time they ship something out of the plant for off-site disposal," comments Mark Kowalski, director of facilities at AeroScientific. The heavy-metal discharges from the old process were reduced to zero.[15]

Hundreds of other case studies demonstrate waste reduction can be economically beneficial and far less troublesome than land disposal. Here are some stunning success stories:

- Cleo-Wrap, the world's largest producer of holiday gift-wrapping paper, is based in Memphis, Tennessee. In 1986, the company completed a six-year conversion project involving the replacement of its organic solvent-based inks with water-based inks. With this step, it reduced its waste-disposal costs by $35,000 a year. Cleo-Wrap also eliminated all underground solvent-storage tanks, thereby avoiding the new federal regulatory system and also lowering fire-insurance premiums by eliminating the fire hazards inherent in the storage and handling of flammable solvents.

• Since 1981, a Borden Chemical plant in Fremont, California, has reduced its discharge of organic sludge into wastewater by ninety-three percent. This was accomplished through a process renovation involving four separate changes in its handling of phenol and urea resins. Simple changes created immense payoffs. Organics were cleaned from filters, new tank-pumping methods were initiated, reactor vessels were rinsed between batches, and transfers between storage and car tanks were altered. Because of these changes, Borden no longer has to rely on controversial on-site evaporation ponds to treat its wastewater.

• A 3M electronics plant in Columbia, Missouri, altered its cleaning of copper sheeting. The change also helped the company's bottom line. Rather than spraying the metal with ammonium persulfate, phosphoric acid, and sulfuric acid, the plant now scrubs the copper in a rotating brush pumice. The plant's generation of liquid hazardous wastes has been reduced by forty thousand pounds per year. In 1985, 3M saved $15,000 in raw materials, disposal, and labor costs. The $59,000 investment paid for itself in three years.

The key to these successes is not just technology, but institutional innovations in management. An organizational structure that puts the environmental dynamic in corporate decision-making is needed in many firms today. A hopeful sign is that various Fortune 500 companies are now preparing corporate officers with the management skills to promote on-site waste-reduction investments.

A recent report presented by Arthur D. Little, Inc., to the 1988 Annual Conference of the National Association of Environmental Professionals, emphasizes how rapidly changes can come about. According to the report, formal auditing programs to monitor environmental, health, and safety risks are becoming common not only within firms here in the United States, but also within their subsidiaries abroad. Senior executives today care not only about compliance with end-of-the-pipe regulations, but also about "appropriate and responsible management of environmental, health, and safety risks." The report adds that while there has been a trend toward cost-cutting and decentralization of companies, most firms have maintained, and more often than not strengthened, departments that deal with hazardous waste.

Edgar S. Woolard, Jr., chief executive officer for Du Pont, now speaks the new corporate language:

"The real environmental challenge is not one of responding to the next regulatory proposal. Nor is it making the environmentalists see things our way. Nor is it educating the public to appreciate the benefits of our products and thus to tolerate their environmental impacts and those of the processes used to make them. Our continued existence as a leading manufacturer requires that we excel in environmental performance and that we enjoy the nonobjection—indeed even the support—of the people and governments in societies where we operate around the world.

"I'm calling for a corporate environmentalism, which I define as an attitude and a performance commitment that places corporate environmental stewardship fully in line with public desires and expectations."

Du Pont, the world's largest manufacturer of chlorofluorcarbons, with $750 million in annual sales, has now promised a complete phaseout of the product by the end of the century. The company has six operating plant facilities designing safer substitutes.[16]

Saving the environment and becoming more efficient translates into a new economic boon. One lesson from Europe is that pollution-control technologies are profitable.[17] According to a report issued by the economics department of Commerzbank, Germany's extremely tough environmental laws have created investment opportunities in the areas of emission controls and waste-disposal equipment that surpass those of all rival nations. Much of the reason for the success, observes the report, is Germany's supportive research-and-development programs. An Organization of Economic Competition and Development study issued in 1988 revealed that West Germany spent 3.3 percent of its public research budget on environmental problems—outdoing the United States, France, and Britain. The Germans even ship desulfurization and denitrification systems to Japan.

America will have to deal with its aging industrial facilities. The new industrial-design goals—reduce waste, conserve energy, save materials—will go far in transforming American industry into a new animal, one that can do more with less. But how long will it take to liberate this new breed? Moreover, what is the role of the average consumer in facilitating the needed change? In the late 1970s, Warren Johnson, chairman of the geography department at San Diego State University, pursued these questions in his book *Muddling Toward Frugality*.[18] René Dubos once commented that Johnson "believes in the resiliency of human beings and sees, in the need to adapt to more frugal ways, the opportunity for new lifestyles that will be happier because they are richer in personal experiences." Johnson's book shows, in short, that the search for environmental excellence does not have to be an enterprise characterized by technological obsessions. Simple common sense, and a return to the satisfying feelings of restraint and self-control, can also reap large-scale rewards.

The logic of frugality runs deep. Johnson observes:

> There are indications that as we move toward the last part of this century, we are beginning to learn some important lessons in the same painful way: Affluence cannot increase indefinitely; technology does not have an answer for all shortages; the march of progress may be taking us in the wrong direction.
>
> The big advantage of the resource issues we are facing is that they are less ambiguous than those of the Depression or the Vietnam War. Shortages are real, in hard, physical terms.

Trying to perpetuate the present mode of resource management is becoming increasingly difficult. In a sense, Johnson points out, "We need the restraint provided by resource limitations."

The word *frugal* has taken on a negative connotation in recent times. Yet the origins of the word come from the Latin *frugalior,* which means "useful" or "worthy," and *frux,* meaning "fruitful" or "productive." This word captures the vision America will need to adopt if we are to develop affordable solutions to environmental woes, and if we are to make the most productive use of our resources.

Chapter 6

The Environmental Movement: Pathways to Reform

Many of the major environmental problems we face are truly international in nature. Their solution will require a president who is adept at negotiating with friend and foe alike—a president who is willing to lead on a global scale.

—PRESIDENT GEORGE BUSH

The American environmental movement traces its richly nourished roots to Earth Day, April 21, 1970. Frightening episodes, such as the infamous 1969 Santa Barbara oil spill which dumped 3.25 million gallons over eight hundred square miles of water and shoreline, had alarmed a growing number of citizens. The press began to ask about the health of our nation and planet. As Californians gazed out over the one-hundred-mile stretch of coastline covered with the suffocating spill, the first wave of grassroots activity on the West Coast broke. *Life* magazine's photographs of thousands of birds, mammals, and fish smothered by Union Oil's black gold were forever imprinted in the public's mind.

When people saw news reports showing how babies in Manhattan and Chicago were breathing air so dirty that the particulates showed up on their white clothes, the public grew more alarmed. And when Lake Erie caught on fire in 1970, a national movement crystallized and enlisted citizens obsessed with a mission: to cast judgments, by force of law, against the perpetrators of these crimes against the earth.

This emphasis on a legal battle waged on behalf of our natural resources was reinforced by the first head of the Environmental Protection Agency, William Ruckelshaus. A lawyer, his number-one priority was the enforcement of the law. Our notions of environmental justice continue to focus on a legal response to a series of specific, fragmented laws that trace their heritage to Earth Day.[1] Groups such as the Natural Resources Defense Council, the Sierra Club, and the Audubon Society continue to spend immense sums of money on suing government and industry. Throwing the law books at polluters, however, is only one part of the answer.

What would a more complete answer to the environmental challenge look like? Rather than being characterized by the stuffiness of courtrooms or the elite liberal coffee klatches of New York or San Francisco, the movement's next wave will be motivated by a set of down-to-earth managerial concerns that simply states that pollution is stupid. Many citizens of all walks of life across the globe are ready to pound their fists and say no to toxics in the workplace or in their homes. Rather than the longwinded plodding and sidestepping arguments of the legal assault, working-class people take quick action when threatened. They sense one can win some games only with a full-court frontal assault.

Profiles in Courage

There have been many heroes in the long and often perilous fight to save the environment. One of the truly remarkable stories is that of Lois Gibbs, who helped make the words *Love Canal* a symbol of a nation's awakening to the horrors of toxics in our neighborhoods.

Fifteen years ago, Lois was living in Love Canal—a favorite spot for honeymooners visiting Niagara Falls. She was living the classic American dream: a mortgaged home, two kids, a white picket fence. Her husband, like many of her neighbors, worked at a local factory that had been well established for years. Suddenly, her son Michael mysteriously contracted asthma, epilepsy, and a liver disease. Michelle, her daughter, then came down with a rare blood disease similar to hemophilia. After struggling with questions about whether she might be to blame, Lois discovered that the factory in town had buried over twenty thousand tons of toxic chemicals in a former dump that rested beneath her children's school. She became convinced that these poisons had manifested themselves in her children's ailments.[2]

After discovering this tragedy, the Gibbs family couldn't move. They couldn't leave this episode behind. No one would buy their home. They had built their whole lives around this community, so they decided to stay and fight. Lois soon discovered that many of the children in her immediate neighborhood had cancer. She was certain that this was no coincidence.

Inventing tactics that have now become standard practice, Lois enlisted local community groups and the media to take on the owners of the polluting factory, the Hooker Chemical Company. The company owners and state and national government officials, however, all denied that there was a problem. They recalculated the scientific figures, adjusting them so that the child cancer rate was closer to politically acceptable nationwide averages. Even churches became part of the indifferent response. While seeking sanctuary for her children, Lois was turned away by her church because the church elders depended upon a major chemical manufacturer for funds.

Ultimately, her anger and persistence paid off. After three years of struggling, Lois was successful in getting the entire community tested for possible contamination. When these tests supported her claims, the entire town made the history books. Some of the area was condemned and hundreds of longtime residents were evacuated. Today, a forty-acre clay cover shrouds the once-vibrant city of Love Canal, a stark symbol and a palpable reminder of the cost of past mistakes.

Lois proved that you can "fight city hall" and win. Today, she is director of the Citizens Clearinghouse for Hazardous Waste, a national organization based in Arlington, Virginia, with fourteen thousand members willing and eager to work in return for nothing more than a safer environment and peace of mind. Lois has become a lightning rod for citizens who too often feel that they are powerless to stop the seemingly endless problems at America's ten thousand leaking landfills.

She notes that most of the people she works with are a different breed from the professional environmentalists that work Capitol Hill. "These professional environmentalists do not want to tackle any issue that challenges the fundamental, cozy relationships between industry and government," complains Lois. They are compromised, she feels, by their preoccupation with middle-of-the-road concerns such as emission controls and other regulatory fine-tuning. The people Lois works with, typically of low or moderate income with high school degrees, see such controls as "a severe compromise." They are interested in out-and-out prevention.

She sees herself as a "popularist," one who talks to real people, not programs, helping to generate "a second wave of environmental reform that moves beyond legal remedies." She recites the following analogy to describe the differences between the professional and grassroots environmentalist: There are two kinds of frogs in a water pot. As the water is heated, one frog—the environmental professional—adjusts his or her biological clock and continually compromises until the water boils, and the frog is cooked. In contrast, the other frog, the grassroots environmentalist mother with her child, does not compromise and jumps out of the water from the start.[3]

Survival is always a supreme motivator. Even the best-intentioned institutions breed complacency.

Approximately ninety percent of the people Lois works with come from blue-collar families, and their success is dependent upon "the power of anger and fear" and the fact that these crusades are "unpredictable." "I'm really not an environmentalist," she says, "I am just fighting for the right of people to choose, for justice. I really don't care about the birds or the trees. The question is: Do we want to drink contaminated water? I am trying to help to fight for the right to make that choice."[4]

Across the Potomac River from Gibbs's office lies the nation's capital, the stomping grounds for one of the nation's most colorful public servants, Hugh Kaufmann. *Newsweek* called him "Idaho's favorite son" for his work opposing the siting of low-level radioactive waste in remote countryside sites. His is the story of a government bureaucrat who has bucked the system, taken the heat, and proved that there is life after whistle-blowing. Kaufmann is the EPA's conscientious objector, and his career teaches several inspiring lessons about the search for environmental excellence.

The son of a career public servant, Kaufmann is familiar with the ins and outs of Washington, D.C. He has had his phone tapped, been trailed by federal agents, and has almost lost his job on more than one occasion. His leaks to the press and his stubborn honesty helped topple the embarrassing programs of EPA administrators Anne Burford and Rita Lavelle, Reagan appointees who lost their jobs under charges of perjury and corruption. He regularly helps citizen grassroots groups by generating media coverage of toxic-waste violations in people's backyards. Along with his successes come the disappointments. The comprehensive Superfund law that he helped draft, and which theoretically could force companies to pay sizable damages for polluting, has never been fully enforced.

The most important lesson of Kaufmann's career is that most important environmental policy decisions are not made at the EPA. Enforcement capabilities are often clipped, says Kaufmann, by a White House that realizes that lax enforcement of the environmental laws is important to major campaign contributors. These contributors, some of the most powerful corporate executives in the country, feel Superfund's penalties are too severe and that its impact will hurt American competitiveness. As to whose is the strongest voice behind environmental decisions, Kaufmann claims it is no secret: it is that of big business. The clout of whistle-blowers[5] can't match the influence of those parked in corporate limousines. Often parked outside the offices of OMB, across the street from the White House, these well-polished icons of how Washington works inspire Kaufmann's wrath.

So, Kaufmann continues. His type of notoriety would make him "unemployable in Europe. If I lived in Russia, I might even be dead." In spite of the friction with annoyed bosses, Kaufmann offers his advice to two to three grassroots groups across the country every month. Such activism from a federal bureaucrat is "the least a good civil servant can do," comments Kaufmann. "The citizens are armed with rubber bands and chewing gum against major polluters armed with the best-paid engineers and lawyers in the country. It ain't a fair fight."

Kaufmann, like Lois Gibbs, has witnessed the building momentum of the next wave of environmental activism. In towns such as Lima and Louisberg, Ohio; Staples, Minnesota; Rockport, Missouri; and Auburn, Nebraska, Kaufmann regularly draws crowds of between three hundred and eight hundred people, the majority of whom are farmers and two-income working-class families concerned about their livelihoods. "These people are the silent majority that Richard Nixon spoke about. These are the real environmentalists. The people who pay taxes and do all the work of America. They don't drive fancy cars or read *Women's Wear Daily*."

Though he recognizes the limits of the legal remedy and the "limousine liberal" label that haunts some environmental causes, Kaufmann also feels the focus on Washington, D.C., is a pardonable practice that reflects the importance of our nation's capital in setting international trends in managing the environment. "People come to Washington, D.C., because of its tremendous resource base here and because everybody, including the Japanese, keys on U.S. decisions." Every major international development firm puts more money into lobbyists in Washington, D.C., than into any other capital in the world.

In reaction to this high-stakes power struggle, "Environmentalists staked out a specific turf in the 1970s," observed Kaufmann. "They exerted their influence on existing law to get the ball moving in the right direction and they devoted most of their resources to legal remedies." This emphasis on legal nitpicking, however, has resulted in the lack of a major environmental agenda for concerned citizens to follow. Kaufmann views this absence of an agenda as the reason he is in such demand.

Next to the whistle-blowers, there are private watchdog groups who, though they frequently focus on legal challenges, play a critical part in the search for environmental protection.[6] A prime example can be seen in the case of the EPA's footdragging on publishing regulations for land disposal of hazardous wastes. The immense importance of these government rules, which were not published until close to six years after congressional mandates requested them, is underscored by the fact that approximately eighty percent of hazardous waste has traditionally been dumped into landfills despite common scientific and engineering knowledge that it is the least preferred method of storing or disposing of hazardous waste.

In stepped the Environmental Defense Fund (EDF), which took advantage of the citizen-suit provision in the Resource Conservation and Recovery Act (RCRA) of 1976 and successfully won a court judgment forcing EPA to issue the regulations. Though the EPA consistently missed its own deadlines, and filed repeated delaying motions, continual vigilance on the part of the EDF (termed "deadline litigation" by those in the trenches) resulted in the publishing of regulations in mid-June 1982. Even then, however, the EDF's work was not done. They reentered the courtroom the following fall, arguing that the regulations were too weak and ineffective to cure the problem.

One of the most gratifying successes of citizen groups not just in America but around the globe has been the termination of ocean incineration of toxic liquids.[7] A key battleground in this fight was the Texas coast, since the first American site for the burning of toxics in furnaces on boats was in the Gulf of Mexico. In 1985, the American government contracted the largest waste handler in the world, Chemical Waste Management, to experiment off the Brownsville docks with trial burns of PCBs, Agent Orange, and other high-risk toxins from old military and petrochemical operations.

The genesis of the campaign against ocean incineration in Texas was a meeting between several high school science teachers who, utilizing their expertise and their belief in the rights of access in a democracy, began to educate neighbors about the hazards of burning chlorinated wastes at sea. Their efforts culminated in the gathering of seventeen thousand signatures of protest. These signatures were then hand-delivered to the head of the Environmental Protection Agency in Washington, D.C., as a declaration of environmental independence.

The successful battle to ban ocean incineration off of U.S. coasts proves, says Joan Brotman of the Gulf Coast Coalition for Public Health, that "if citizens do their homework, and pull their scientific information together, they have power." She noted that two ocean-incineration hearings about proposed Gulf Coast burns drew over ten thousand people "in a rural community where you put a sign up, and many of the people can't even read it."

Among those who joined the effort to ban ocean incineration is Shirley Goldsmith of Lake Charles, Louisiana. She got involved with ocean incineration and other environmental causes because "The air was so bad here. It was waking me up every morning at three o'clock. I got tired of nobody doing anything about it." Goldsmith noted that Lake Charles falls in what is commonly called the "cancer alley" of the Deep South, and that several of her close friends had died mysteriously, prompting her to start poking around to find the cause. Sadly, she has had to curtail her activism because of declining health allegedly brought on by toxic contamination.[8]

Joining Goldsmith in the crusade to stop ocean incineration was Jacques Cousteau, who through fifty years of activism has on numerous occasions wisely summed-up our environmental predicament. "The sickness of the ocean has its origins in our heredity; ignorance, superstition, thirst for individual power. The diagnosis points to uncontrolled proliferation and growth, a disease of the cancer family. The cancer that plagues the ocean is our cancer," he said in 1980. "We should realize that there is only one problem, that of survival. We forget that the water cycle and the life cycle are one. Environment is one, too. There is no such thing as the environment of a single species—of man, for example, or of a town, a locality. The only environment is the environment of life."

Activists such as Cousteau, citizens such as Goldsmith, and organizations such as the Gulf Coast Coalition did not stop there. They wanted to become part of the answer and advocated better alternatives for the wastes.[9] As a result of their efforts, many European and American firms are now redesigning their manufacturing processes to either reuse or destroy the same wastes on-site. The lesson is simple. When citizens close off a suspect activity, they often create enough pressure for serious innovation and improvement to occur. Citizens are an increasingly important part of environmental answers, complementing the market-dominated debates of science and law.

Pardonable Practices

Although environmentalists have made significant progress in making the world cleaner and safer, their tactics can also backfire.

Environmentalists such as the anarchistic "deep ecologists" of Earth First![10] (who suggested that the solution to the Ethiopian famine was "just to let nature seek its own balance") sometimes cause more harm than good. They polarize potential environmental allies and deny the need to bring together environmentalists, government leaders, and industrial innovators. When the co-founder of Earth First! says, "I will fight every industrial proposal until there are as many grizzly bears in the Bay Area as Americans,"[11] one can hardly claim that he is trying to build an agenda that generates broad support.

There is no doubt that the globetrotting tactics of radical groups such as Greenpeace, who continually expose outrageous clandestine activities by major polluters on the high seas, and who are willing to risk their lives to stop the senseless killing of whales, are an important part of the equation when it comes to environmental reform. These activists may prove to be this century's equivalent to the perpetrators of the Boston Tea Party, announcing a newer and safer order. Nonetheless, it is important to recognize that yelling "Fire!" in a crowded room is just the first step. One also has to point out which doors can be used for escape.[12]

Scanning the literature on environmental abuse, a few dominant analysts and writers emerge. Michael Brown, who broke the story on Lois Gibbs and Love Canal, exemplifies the sustained intensity of crisis journalism. His research has documented a host of environmental disasters: eight hundred pounds of chemical residues from industrial lagoons washing into Lake Michigan after heavy rainstorms; underground toxic vapors venting alongside occupied trailer homes in Anaheim, California; the explosion of hundreds of drums of lead, mercury, arsenic, and nitroglycerine illegally stacked in a toxic waste dump in Elizabeth, New Jersey. Without crisis journalism spotlighting these cases, we might not have many of the new toxics regulations on the books. When statistics demonstrate, nevertheless, that less than half of America's businesses are complying with these regulations, one has to pause and ponder whether this single-minded, crisis-driven regulatory approach to environmental reform is enough.[13]

Brown's solution is to "fine the hell out of corporations" so that it becomes uneconomical to pollute. He hardly sympathizes with the compliance challenges before the Environmental Protection Agency. Brown once proclaimed: "It is the EPA's job to stop persistent and carcinogenic chemicals from debasing the quality of life—human, animal, and plant life alike. Period. Whatever that entails as far as the convoluted regulations go is EPA's business—or should be."

Sympathetic critics of the environmental movement, such as the popular journalist William Tucker, contest Brown's brazen approach. They argue that reforms need to be based on the market, not pie-in-the-sky regulations which state impractical goals without regard to modern business limits.[14] One illustration of Tucker's worries about an overemphasis on regulatory zeal comes from California. In a study of hazardous-waste government reporting forms, it was revealed that California businesses collectively filled out an average of sixteen hundred forms per day just to comply with one aspect of the state's environmental law: the Resource Conservation and Recovery Act.

What's worse, Robert Powell, a chemical-engineering professor at the University of California–Davis, found that less than fifty percent of the eleven thousand forms he analyzed in research on hazardous-waste generation in California were complete. Only 23.5 percent of the information on these forms was considered correct. These figures call into question the value of relying on regulations and paperwork to solve the toxics dilemma.

"The more I examine the environmental movement," observes Tucker, "the more it seems like a kind of secular religion, with a decidedly Puritan strain. Like all religious movements, it draws its strength from what we don't know." He goes on to say that he worries that historians looking back will shake their heads at the present environmental movement. "We are going to appear as a generation that was so obsessed with misgivings, so afraid of what we didn't—and couldn't—know, so anxious to point hysterical accusing fingers at one another, that we neglected to pick up and use the simple tools we had at hand."

Tucker, in spite of his insightful analysis of the environmental schizophrenia[15] that exists in America, doesn't hold out much hope for progress and views the environmental movement as an impediment, rather than an ally, in promoting industrial revitalization. What Tucker overlooks is that people can rapidly redirect business by voting with their pocketbooks. The power of boycotts has been waged effectively more than once. As the economic incentives for recycling increase, reuse of metals, plastic, glass, and paper will become habit for future generations—just as it was during the World Wars. Already, consumers are telling their favorite fast-food or local sandwich shop that Styrofoam cups, produced with ozone-depleting CFCs, are unwanted.

Tucker's cynical observations offer a useful challenge for the

THE FORK IN THE ROAD

I. Adversarial Politics

  A. End-pipe regulations

  B. Legal litigation for problem solving

  C. Enforcement and fines

II. Consumer Society

  A. Inability to distinguish between wants and needs

  B. Materialism: the American Dream

  C. Reliance on the superabundance and resilience of nature

III. Dominant Culture

  A. Nationalism's inability to act

  B. Creator/destroyer attitude

  C. Short-term usage

I. Beyond Blame

  A. Solution orientation

  B. Building from a common ground

  C. Education and development funding

II. Less Is More

  A. Self-sufficiency and minimalism

  B. Conservation values toward natural resources

  C. Environmental and resource management

III. Emergent Culture

  A. Global perspective; grassroots activism

  B. Living as an implicit part of nature

  C. Long-term planning

Source: Assembled by Chris Hynes for American Hazard Control Group

next wave of environmental reformers. What he fails to grasp in his analysis, however, is that the environmental movement is not yet sufficiently market-based, the market is fed by basic working-class people, and their values may push the movement beyond the confines of "secular religion" and into the living rooms of everyday life.

A Most Elaborate Masquerade

In its drama and antics, environmental advocates often employ the complex art of masquerade. Past cases of environmental neglect are recast in a more colorful present in order to create a better tomorrow. This "masking" phenomenon, whereby the ordinary concerns of health and safety are rendered extraordinary for widespread impact, links environmentalists with the full catalogue of mass social movements of the last two centuries. From the nineteenth-century labor movement to the present women's rights movement, people have painted themselves to gather attention and build momentum for their cause.

From up close, any single-minded zest or set of unorthodox manners of expression seems odd, like the bizarre eye makeup of a Mardi Gras participant. Seen from a distance, however, the getup has a fantastic and theatrical effect. This feature of sportive seriousness is hardly confined to environmental advocates. It is a common strategy for effecting social change. In *The True Believer,* the longshoreman Eric Hoffer states: "All mass movements generate in their adherents a readiness to die and a proclivity for united action; all of them, irrespective of the doctrine they preach and the program they project, breed fanaticism, enthusiasm, fervent hope, hatred and intolerance; all of them are capable of releasing a powerful flow of activity in certain departments of life; all of them demand blind faith and single-hearted allegiance."

Though Hoffer carefully differentiates these beliefs, his book claims that a common human pattern drives "the fanatical Mohammedan, the fanatical nationalist, the fanatical Communist, the fanatical Nazi, and the fanatical Christian." Moreover, Hoffer warns that "the true believer is everywhere on the march, and both by converting and antagonizing, he is shaping the world in his own image."

Everything Hoffer says about mass movements is evident in the modern environmental movement. In addition, a finer point needs to be made: strong social movements based as much on fear as on technical concerns and specific political agendas often attract fringe components. The situation in the environmental movement is, once again, not unlike that of the Mardi Gras. In addition to the grand splendor and legitimate fun, there are some thieves and vagabonds[16] present who prey upon the extravagant show. These fringe elements capitalize on the distraction of the event, the way a corporation may choose to capitalize on a contaminated worker's need for a job during a worker-safety negotiation.

When fringe elements subvert the ongoing masquerade for lesser purposes, the public-policy process sometimes aborts. The resulting paralysis is now staring environmentalists in the face on issues not only of waste management but of new energy sources.[17] The true test for American environmentalism is to achieve a better balance between fear of ecological catastrophe and trust in our political system. We have a legitimate fear about our industrial past.

The road to environmental excellence is not smoothly paved with the certainties of science, nor clearly marked by a legalistic black-and-white view of what's ahead. The desire for an easy ride in the search for answers will often be frustrated by confusion and fears. In response, the technocratic elite may propose to repave the road in order to give the issue the appearance of certainty.

Nonetheless, one cannot forget that it is normal to be suspicious of strontium-90 or other radioactive fallout; it makes basic sense to distrust chlorinated hydrocarbons such as Agent Orange, DDT, or PCBs. Environmental protesters, from this vantage point, have plenty of good reasons to masquerade. Television is often the best way to circumvent the cumbersome legislative process. Since the path of legislation is often only available to those with expensive road maps and lavish lobbying resources, the cheaper route of immediate media attention is a sensible one to take.

Luckily, Hollywood, scene of what is perhaps the most influential masquerade on earth, has suddenly discovered the environment, and the 1990s will therefore increasingly be shaped by ecological values. Cynics may feel this turn of events is just a reflection of another moneymaking fad,[18] but the truth is undeniable. When a starlet like Madonna, who once sang the virtues of shopping in "Material Girl," becomes a fervent advocate of halting deforestation, her message will be widely broadcast. "Every second, an area the size of a football field is gone—forever. At this rate, the entire rain forest will be gone in fifty years—forever. The forests give us life; we've got to find a way to preserve them," said Madonna at a 1989 "Don't Bungle the Jungle" fundraiser in New York City.

The turning point for the entertainment industry was 1986 and California Proposition 65, an initiative designed to give citizens the right to hold industry accountable for 250 cancer-causing chemicals that have been found in drinking water by shifting the burden of proof from citizen to corporation. Actress Jane Fonda—along with members of the "Brat Pack" and a host of other Hollywood celebrities—traveled up and down the California coastline publicizing the cause. Even though the initiative supporters were heavily outspent by national oil companies, the measure won.

One of the main forces behind the "Get Tough on Toxics" Proposition—California Assemblyman Tom Hayden—is now back at it again with an initiative for 1990 that is the most comprehensive piece of environmental legislation in U.S. history. Weaving several incremental changes into a strategic whole, the measure could just ride the crest of the new wave of environmentalism breaking from coast to coast.

Ironically, it is the conversion of Hollywood's liberal elite to the environment that may prove to be the critical bridge to blue-collar Americans. The key behind-the-scenes player in Hollywood is Norman Lear, producer of "All in the Family" and a firm believer in the power of television to shape attitudes. Other Hollywood figures, such as entertainment lawyer Bonnie Reiss, have already formed groups such as Earth Communications Office. Its mission: to recruit producers, directors, and writers to weave ecological values into tomorrow's soap operas, sitcoms, and even Saturday-morning cartoons.

Once one accepts the strategy of a masquerade, much of what at first appears to be a great deal of groping and wasted energy takes on a new value. This waste, which is even evident among professional environmentalists, is useful, since it provides an important sense of social purpose to Americans entering the twenty-first century. The environmental masquerade provides individuals with a sense of participation in groups while the rest of society seems to be raising more and more barriers between human beings. The fulfillment derived by the environmentalist who mobilizes his or her neighbors to join in is a substantial reward in today's increasingly impersonal and automated world. Environmental threats may be one of the few things that members of a community have in common. A mutual enemy is always an effective stimulus.

The dread of toxic contamination, coupled with the lack of trust in government and industry, speaks to a wellspring of common sense which feeds the environmental movement. As we near the end of this troubled century, a basic responsibility of government is, above all else, to provide security and peace. Financial rewards may soon appear secondary to these two basic needs. The growing popularity of the environmental movement is a natural function of people expressing their desires to restore some security to their lives.

The fundamental desire for security is the lasting impetus behind the next wave of environmentalism. It will not be based on uncommon science or esoteric law, but instead, on managerial common sense. The fears and hopes of ordinary folk in everyday life are real and are taking center stage. The second wave of environmentalism will be a visceral, as well as practical, response to these everyday needs.[19]

The Link with Labor

Among the globe's many social movements, the environmental movement finds its most compelling parallel in labor movements. The common link between these at-times separate developments is the role of women in both.

Though labor groups and environmentalists have frequently been found on opposite sides of the fence on such issues as nuclear power (a favorite bumpersticker reads: HUNGRY? OUT OF WORK? EAT AN ENVIRONMENTALIST!) the resilience of both movements, and their sharing of the same major adversary—big business—speak to a kinship in style as well as substance.

For reasons far more basic than those implied by statistical surveys or feminist tracts, women have often taken the lead in worker-safety issues. Some of the earliest demonstrations against unsafe working conditions occurred in textile mills in Lowell and Manchester, Massachusetts, in the 1830s and 1840s. Now one of the nation's major Superfund sites, the mill in Lowell was the setting where over a hundred female workers defied their society's submissive image of women by walking off the job in protest. Sweatshops all across the country, which factory women often helped build, became hotbeds of organized protest against inhumane working conditions. Better working conditions often mean better environmental management.

In the early twentieth century, some of the nation's first heavy industries popped up in the Mohawk Valley, stretching from Amsterdam to Albany, New York. Here too women were delegated the work that no one else wanted to do for low pay and long hours. The inhumanity of these working conditions was shocking and now highlights the progress that has been made in upgrading many business practices. The fact that current environmentalists are continuing the fight for a less toxic workplace is proof of the common bond shared by labor and environmentalists.

Women's struggle for dignity and justice aided the causes of labor and environmental safety simultaneously. Throughout the late nineteenth and twentieth centuries, it was typically women who noticed how antiquated and inefficient many of the industrial machines then in use had become. Among the more notorious protesters were the "Rebel Girls," who were led by Elizabeth Gurley Flynn. During the winter of 1912, she led the female mill-workers on a strike that resulted in the eventual modernization of mills.

The significant point about labor leaders advocating environmentalist causes is that the second wave of modern environmentalism will be rooted in the working class. Activists will come from the workers in England, Italy, and Spain, not just the rich of the United States, Scandinavia, and Central Europe. The factory workers of the world have the most to complain about, and often the most to lose in terms of environmental contamination.

Unlike labor struggles of the past, however, this next wave of environmentalism will include business leaders who realize that safer workplaces and more efficient machines make good business sense. Along with these corporate leaders are a growing number of businesses that have profited from the continuous evolution of hazardous-waste management laws. People such as Lawrence Cahill of Hart Environmental Management have provided many Fortune 500 companies with assistance in complying with new hazardous waste management laws.

Through use of environmental audits, Cahill and many like him work to ensure that industries assume a more active role in addressing possible environmental disasters. "We subscribe to Murphy's law," notes Cahill, a toxic mishap is an event that today's companies need to prepare for. It is not that unusual, according to Cahill, for some firms to run emergency-response drills at two or three o'clock in the morning—and if a plant manager fails to respond adequately, he or she may be fired.

Because many companies are becoming leaner and meaner in today's competitive business environment—trying, as Cahill puts it, "to do more with less"—corporations are relying more and more on outside experts to work intermittently on toxic problems. When consultants are brought on board just for specific projects, payrolls devoted to environmental compliance are reduced.

From Cahill's vantage point, the environmental movement has been successful in "providing a point on the lever" to help tip society toward practical solutions of environmental problems. "After all, we are all people, just trying to live on this planet," observes Cahill. The noise created by environmental groups balances out the views of special interests who continually push their own agendas to the detriment of long-term resource protection goals.

Cahill's major criticism has been leveled at the approach government regulators have taken in response to environmentalists. By mandating health and safety standards which, all told, number approximately nine thousand, government now focuses on the strict, rigid interpretation of these rules. "The fact of the matter is that regulators are bureaucrats who don't get out into the real world situation enough. They operate inside a black box. For instance, the EPA tries to mandate rules to cover every case of a certain type of problem when every case is different," says Cahill. Instead, the agency should be more open to negotiate the inevitable variables.

The theme of developing a more flexible approach to hazardous waste management is echoed by George Vander Velde of Chemical Waste Management, Inc., the largest U.S. company devoted to hazardous waste management.[20] Vander Velde is vice president of science and technology at the firm. He also directs the research-and-development activities.

"The sheer volume of regulations, which often conflict, make it very difficult for some companies to understand whether they are in compliance or not," observes Vander Velde. Often, he notes, literal compliance is virtually impossible, particularly "when rules are adopted after the fact" because of EPA footdragging. Therefore, Vander Velde suggests that the regulatory structure needs some fine-tuning to foster more flexible controls and to increase confidence in the system. For instance, environmental rules sometimes require certain wastes to be handled under stringent regulations because of legal definitions and listing, while under different circumstances a company can do anything they want with the same toxin because the substance does not fall under the jurisdiction of Superfund liability. Vander Velde observes that government officials are learning as they go along, and that a maturing of a government response to the toxic crisis is currently underway.

On a more positive note, Vander Velde says that over the past five years, the awareness of hazardous-waste responsibilities has increased dramatically among manufacturing and service companies.

Vander Velde is not quite as generous as Cahill in his assessment of the success of the environmental movement. He highlights improvements in air quality[21] as the most visible sign of progress and admits that the environmentalists have "brought into focus a number of important issues." Just the same, he complains that too often environmentalists "paint all of industry with one brush" and are driven by their "own vested interests and agendas not specifically directed toward environmental betterment."

Vander Velde doesn't foresee the environmental movement focusing too heavily on the concerns of blue-collar families; instead he expects it to continue expanding in "a very broad-based alliance" that harks back to such "primal" concerns as "survival." He remarks, "The environment has become a nonpartisan issue." In addition, the movement has "matured" by shifting its attention from "what" questions to the "where and how" of technical solutions.

Perhaps one reflection of this evolution of the environmental movement is the motto of Rollins Environmental Services, Inc.: "We are not the problem, but part of the solution." As vice president of national sales Richard Sernyak points out, "It is good business sense to be concerned about the environment. We all have a vested interest in it." Describing himself as a "pragmatist on environmental issues," Sernyak argues that "emotionalism serves no real purpose" except to fuel little wars. "It is the business technocrats who, operating within a capitalist framework, roll up their sleeves to solve environmental problems and keep jobs."

Since his introduction to the business of environmental consulting back in 1973, Sernyak has witnessed a major transition from companies handling waste in a "cheap, dumb, and dirty" manner to a new, sophisticated approach that recognizes that those concerned "are the consumers buying the products these corporations produce." Therefore, "Compliance with laws is not enough." His firm utilizes the best available technologies (BAT) to cope with toxic headaches. "You cannot be too clever, too good. You have to be beyond reproach," he proclaims.

He warns, however, that unless a more rational balance exists between environmentalists, government, and industry, "we are on a collision course" that could have lasting repercussions. He points to public opposition to a trash-to-steam project in Philadelphia, his hometown, as an example of how emotionalism can work against environmental solutions. "Because of ignorance and hysteria, citizens do not realize that such a facility would actually result in clean air. All they can see is the plume and they equate that with crisis."

He views the environmental movement from the perspective of five- to ten-year life cycles. Today, he postulates, we are at "the end of the introductory stage of the environmental life cycle" and "are about to embark upon the developmental stage," which is heavily dependent upon our nation's educational system. "Many of today's environmental problems will go away as soon as we can imprint environmental sensitivities and values on our country's youth."

Sernyak sees the unfolding of the environmental movement as a "basic synergy" between all elements of society, including a dissolving of the antagonism between management and labor. He summed it up this way: "It simply makes good business sense to have workers that are healthy, happy, and motivated. The needs of industry are linked to the needs of capitalism, to the needs of government, to the needs of the environment."

People from all walks of life must realize that they are part of the answer. For government to put into place new laws and regulations is just one part of the solution. For example, many environmentalists popped champagne bottles with the news of the establishment of a ban on dumping plastics into the ocean in 1989. The biggest part of this battle, however, is to enforce compliance with this and other new environmental laws while at the same time helping industry find new, cost-effective methods of maintaining financial health.

Even the environmental professionals are aware of the challenge before us. Mike McClosky of the Sierra Club acknowledged the shortcomings of the professional environmental movement given its own present substantial resources. "In the late 1980s, the environmental movement is under attack for having delivered lots of laws and words but not enough results when it comes to improving the physical environment." McClosky suggested that groups, driven by the need to continually tackle new issues to raise funds through mass mailings, should instead narrow their focus. Instead of steamy bombast, groups should be disciplined to develop constructive solutions.

SOME BACKGROUND DATA ON KEY ENVIRONMENTAL
ORGANIZATIONS—1987

Name	Founded	Membership	Total Income
Defenders of Wildlife	1947	78,000	$ 3,637,825
Wilderness Society	1935	160,000	$ 8,606,240
Sierra Club	1892	394,393	$15,727,338
National Wildlife Federation	1936	4,600,000	$59,371,000
Environmental Defense Fund	1967	60,000	$ 4,859,888
Natural Resources Defense Council	1970	65,000	$ 7,504,218
The Nature Conservancy	1951	309,643	$40,782,000

It is easier to stop a mistake than to redirect society's focus and forge a better solution. Yet many Americans are ready for this next phase of environmentalism. They want to be part of the answer. To "just say no" is not enough. One must also build the alternative. An instinct of workmanship, which Thorstein Veblen astutely noted as "conspicuously absent" among the leisure class, will forge tomorrow's environmental solutions.

The Limits of American Environmentalism

Some of the most creative approaches to implementing social change have occurred in Europe, where citizens' groups play an intricate role in environmental policy battles. Since citizens are afforded fewer legal rights than in the United States, European activists have developed a rich set of nonjudicial means of influencing the debates over environmental issues.

In West Germany, where there is no Freedom of Information Act, activists enlist the press to obtain elusive documents; they have developed an even closer relationship with the media than have their counterparts in the United States. The West German approach to hazardous-waste management—with each state drawing up its own guidelines—is a peer-pressure-based model that has utilized individual initiative and regional pride to spur development of some of the most advanced approaches in the world to hazardous-waste management. City managers and local hazardous-waste officials are encouraged to compete in a sort of environmental technology sweepstakes, to see which locale can do the best job.

Grassroots activism plays a very important role in environmental policy formulation, too. The well-known German Green Party traces its roots to the anti–Vietnam War protests of the 1960s and 1970s. It is a loosely knit band of community groups which, united by 1980, totaled fifty thousand members. The deliberate anarchy which dominates the Greens' agenda—no representatives are allowed to serve full terms and so step down at the halfway point—and the continuous drama associated with the movement reinforces earlier observations about the environmental masquerade.

Among the novel policy initiatives that the Greens have helped place on the West German national agenda is the development of an "environmental price" to be placed on labels of goods, informing consumers of the amount of waste generated to create the product, and its relative hazards when compared to other products. Not only does this establish a direct link between consumption and responsibility, but it publicizes an objective gauge of environmental impact based on "toxic emissions per unit of resource used."

Instead of the incessant litigation that characterizes the American environmental tussle, the Germans rely on intense mutual scrutiny between companies and environmental professionals— sort of an extended political debate with the voting public keeping score.

In Holland, environmental groups receive subsidies from local, provincial, and national governments, which frees them from fundraising worries and allows them to concentrate on issue development. (Similar subsidization extends also to civic, political, and artistic endeavors.) On some occasions, the government has even subsidized citizens' legal claims on environmental issues, recognizing that the underlying concerns are warning signals of governmental shortcomings.

Perhaps the best way to contrast the Dutch and the American systems is to describe how the Dutch handled their nation's version of our Love Canal. The small village of Lekkerkerk expanded in the 1970s, and soon residents occupying new housing complained of a variety of maladies, ostensibly brought on by toxic contamination. At the time, there was no public access to planning documents, but some clever town residents obtained government documents that indicated that 1,650 drums of paint and industrial waste had been dumped there. Bypassing local officials (since the local government had taken the unusual step of issuing a retroactive disposal permit without public notice), 130 of the 300 families in town made a direct appeal to the national government and the queen to intervene. Within six months, residents were rapidly evacuated, their homes were purchased at their fair market value (as assessed *before* the threat of contamination), and monies were provided for attorneys and child care.

As we have found, there is much still to learn from nations other than our own.

Moving Beyond Blame

One of the distinguishing features of the environmental movement, now breaking across Eastern Europe, the Soviet Union, and Asia, and mixing with the growing currents in the United States and Western Europe, is its inclusiveness. Men and women, rich and poor, far and near, are all beginning to ask the same set of questions. As they take off their masks and discover that the battle to save the environment is a journey that cuts across all societal divisions, we discover how universal the concerns for environmental health and safety have become. Throughout the 1990s, the primal issue of mobilizing a response to shared global challenges will bind generations, races, and nations, and inspire sustained human interest.

We started this book with an account of our role in the effort to halt ocean incineration. For us, that was an early instance of how unifying the search for environmental excellence would become.

Environmental excellence, moreover, is not just stopping mistakes. It is also the search for better answers, an elaborate spiral of greater efficiency, less waste, and saved materials. Sometimes the pursuit involves subtle reversals of institutional trends, reversals which in small ways inspire considerable improvements.

One of the most surprising examples of excellence we found evolved from the Office of Management and Budget, where Robert K. Dawson supervised all natural-resources, energy, and science budgets and programs. Though quite hidden in his large office in Washington's Executive Office Building, Dawson occupied a premier place among Reagan administration civil servants.

During his 1984 confirmation hearings for the OMB job, Dawson obtained the distinction of being the first nominee in U.S. history to draw formal protests from environmental groups. He calls it, sportively, "confirmation terrorism." Their objections were based on his streamlining of regulations while he managed the budget for the Army Corps of Engineers.

Ironically, two years after being confirmed, Dawson drew praises from the same environmentalists because of the excellence achieved by his sweeping Water Resources Act of 1986. This legislation instituted a fifty-fifty co-funding requirement between the federal and local governments for public works projects such as expanding ports, channelizing streams, and redredging harbors. As a consequence, the coalitions that had supported such projects came apart at the seams and were replaced by new, unexpected alliances of administration leaders, such as David Stockman, working hand in hand with environmental groups to press Congress for reforms. Original "pork barrel" proposals at ports in Baltimore, Maryland; Norfolk, Virginia; Mobile, Alabama; and New Orleans, Louisiana, were significantly scaled down and redesigned with a more thorough environmental analysis. The resulting projects were smaller, created less dredge spoils, and were less disruptive of local ecosystems.

In short, both business and citizen, the environment and government, won. Often the search for environmental excellence requires just such a subtle readjustment of scale, and such an insightful refocusing of institutions.

Environmental excellence is, in addition, more than just belt-tightening. We often found it in places far from the nation's capital. Among the greatest contributions to the search for environmental excellence are the private efforts of businessmen such as Mr. L. W. Schatz of General Plastics Manufacturing Company of Tacoma, Washington. In light of severe budget cuts for renewable-energy research throughout the 1980s, Schatz has decided to donate $150,000 to Humboldt State University—his alma mater—for the development of an energy system which offers a vision of the future. The 8-kilowatt demonstration project, a product of private initiative, will enlist the help of university graduate students and is now attracting the interest of utilities such as Pacific Gas & Electric. The project hopes to demonstrate that a PV-hydrogen economy is a viable energy option for the United States. Under the envisioned scenario, huge solar farms in the Southwest would harness the energy of the sun through a process known as electrolysis. This energy would be stored in hydrogen, which could be contained in fuel cells, and used to power vehicles. It could also heat homes by being pumped through modified natural-gas lines.

Examples of excellence abound, and sometimes they simply require a fresh look to the past. Even the junkman, formerly the scorn of most neighborhoods, is being enlisted in the search for environmental excellence. Take Schnitzer Steel of Oakland, California, a company that started recycling steel some seventy years ago. The recent recipient of local business awards, Schnitzer, like the other metal recyclers located in California, has the attitude necessary to tackle the environmental challenge.

When California in 1983 adopted the strictest laws on hazardous waste in the world, Schnitzer and others responded by developing a new technique that bonds the molecules of metal residues, stabilizing them so securely that they can be safely land-disposed. While Gary Schnitzer's initial reaction had been to see the new state regulations as an unfair burden, he soon viewed it in a new light. "Firms such as ours may not be as competitive as other companies in the other forty-nine states because we have additional costs that other shredders do not have, but we have something more important—peace of mind. And that is worth a fortune," says Schnitzer.

Companies such as Schnitzer generate 100,000 tons of metals for reuse every year. But the firm is not yet satisfied. Indeed, they are helping the entire metals recycling industry push for a "Design for Recycling" program, an initiative that hopes to cut down on landfill wastes by forcing manufacturers of products to think about what will happen to their products after they are discarded.

The greatest test in furthering the search for environmental excellence will be the teaching of environmental management to the next generation. An early example of this kind of educational program is the adopt-a-beach concept, which got its start in Texas in October 1986. The tradition of dumping garbage at sea had resulted in a disgusting accumulation of debris on the coast that not only offended sensibilities, but was having an impact on tourism. A 172-mile stretch of accessible Texas coast was broken up into segments about a mile long and adopted by some 130 different groups who promise to clean up three times a year. During the first three sweeps, some 15,300 volunteers picked up 579.25 tons of garbage.

The concept has now spread to other states, including California, and is being utilized by various schools to teach youngsters the value of recycling. This has already resulted in instances where schoolchildren have lectured littering adults about the values of conservation. "We must start educating people at a young age about the importance of conservation and recycling," says Margaret Elliott of the Oceanic Society. "Our goal is to have the lessons learned today about ocean pollution and recycling stay with the children for the rest of their lives. We want to instill in the next generation of leaders and citizens a strong conservation and recycling ethic that will translate into a cleaner and safer environment."

This book has been assembled to further this momentum toward excellence, a force expressed by the actions of thousands of specialists, entrepreneurs, and citizens every day. Someday soon, these efforts will break down the myths that for far too long have kept the industrialized world relatively inactive concerning the environment. The remarkable good news is that by Earth Day 1990 the top managers of the worlds of finance, industry, and the media are now fueling the elaborate search for answers.

Afterword:
Getting to Solutions

My experience over nearly two decades in both the legislative and executive branches of the U.S. government has shown me that the process for dealing with environmental problems actually changes little from one administration to the next, despite what one hears in the news. America's environmental policy has never been set by one individual or one agency, and will not be in the future. Instead, environmental policy reflects a broad bipartisan public involvement. In addition, policy implementation is shaped by a wide range of public and private institutions. What needs to change significantly is the quality and realism of that process. This book points us firmly and persuasively in that direction.

The environmental community, to its credit, now often supports the idea of including costs in some environmental decisions. A case in which I played a role concerned cost-sharing for federal water projects. Traditionally, administrations, environmental groups, and many in the Congress have opposed water projects whose costs exceeded their benefits. Until a bill requiring enhanced nonfederal cost-sharing for federal water projects was enacted in 1986, localities that benefited from uneconomic water projects had no real reason to oppose them. Now that state and local governments must pay a significant share of the costs, local sponsors see these projects in a new, more efficient light.

The results are what Piasecki and Asmus aptly characterize as a search for excellence. The size of individual water projects is now often scaled down to more economical dimensions. Downsizing of authorized projects has already saved the federal government tens of millions of dollars at the Baltimore, Norfolk, Mobile, and New Orleans harbors. This has meant significantly less disruption to the land and water affected by these projects. Society as a whole has benefited both from an environmental-protection and budget standpoint, as the size, cost, and environmental impact of water projects are driven down by the reality of cost-sharing.

Environmental groups could do more, in my opinion, to advance and finance the search for excellence. These groups at times diminish their credibility, their vitally important role in the policy-development process, and distort the results of the process itself, when they fail to base policy recommendations on balanced and affordable programs.

While I was in charge of the U.S. Army Corps of Engineers, and later as associate director of the U.S. Office of Management and Budget with responsibility for policy and budget in the areas of natural resources, energy, and science, I often witnessed environmentalists putting too much effort into second-guessing engineering decisions and trying to force the expenditure of large sums of money to achieve relatively small cleanup benefits in one specific arena at the expense of all others. Experience has shown in many cases that the first ninety-five percent of pollutants can be cleaned up more cheaply than the remaining five percent. Accordingly, the public can often be best served by settling for ninety-five-percent cleanup in a particular site, and using the resources saved on the remaining five percent on more important environmental causes.

I see the shift toward individual citizen involvement and economic realism in environmental decision-making as a healthy development. In the past, the public has been largely shielded from the trade-offs inherent in risk management. People have tended to neglect the complex agreements required of government and industry to make environmental protection work. Most people have little awareness that the public, not industry, actually bears most of these costs through higher product prices and, sometimes, through lost jobs. Faced with little or no perceived cost, it is no wonder that the public tends to want zero-risk solutions that are often neither feasible nor cost-beneficial.

Unfortunately, too many environmental issues are decided

based on emotion rather than reason. In fact, many common risks we accept in everyday life are much more grave than some environmental risks that are subject to intense federal, state, and local regulation. To the extent that we can convince individuals that we live in a world of limited resources and that risk management is the proper approach to environmental decision-making, the better our policy decisions will be and the better off we will be as a society, regardless of who the ultimate or newsworthy policymakers are. This book, aptly subtitled *Moving Beyond Blame,* goes far in articulating this timely sentiment.

Even if one does not agree with everything Piasecki and Asmus write, I believe all readers will recognize in this book perceptive insights into some of the most difficult problems ever to face mankind. This country and the world need such insights and need the wisdom of this book.

—Honorable Robert K. Dawson
1990

Notes

CHAPTER 1

1. For a more sustained and scholarly examination of America's trust in nature, see Piasecki, *Walt Whitman and The American Estimate of Nature: A Study in the Rhetoric of Environmental Reform* (PhD thesis, Cornell University, 1981).
2. For an excellent, up-to-date scientific account of nature's "healing limits," see *Recovery and Restoration of Damaged Ecosystems.* Published by University Press of Virginia and edited by ecologist J. Cairns, Jr., biologist K. L. Dickson, and civil engineer E. E. Herricks, this twenty-one-article collection reviews humankind's recent experience in engineering restoration projects. From an estuary in London to damaged lakes in Sweden, from streams recovering from acid mine drainage to rocky seashores recovering from North Sea oil spills, this text outlines the healing limits of a wide range of natural settings. Today, ecologists call this field of study "assimilative capacity analysis." We choose to retain the original, more humanistic insinuations in the phrase "healing limits."
3. For a fuller argument about the environmental planning challenge still before us in the Great Plains, see the Poppers' "A Daring Proposal for Dealing with an Inevitable Disaster," in *Smithsonian,* December 1987.
4. For a historical account of environmentally induced health crises, see Martin V. Melosi's *Garbage in Cities,* published by Texas A&M Press in 1981.
5. The U.S. EPA and Environment Canada have co-published a useful and attractive booklet entitled *The Great Lakes: An Environmental Atlas and Resource Book.* With excellently written and thoroughly researched chapters, this 44-page booklet is the best "quick look" at the environmental challenges facing the Great Lakes. The cartography, incidentally, is quite beautiful also.
6. For an explanation of these policy challenges, please see: *Alternatives: Perspectives on Society, Technology and Environment,* vol. 13, no. 3 (special issue: *Saving the Great Lakes,* Sept.–Oct. 1986).
7. Those interested in learning more about toxic air emissions might wish to read Michael Brown's *The Toxic Cloud* (New York: Pantheon, 1986).
8. In coining the phrase "senile capitalism," we mean nothing mean-spirited or socially misdirected. We intend, instead, to focus attention on the remarkable forgetfulness of modern-day economic decision-making.

   In its origins, the word "economy" and the word "ecology" derived their rich and timely meanings from the Greek word for home—*oikos.* Once, the idea of the science of our natural setting and the idea of managing our resources were seen as fundamentally related, not opposed. The conceptual bankruptcy of modern economics—where terms like *bottom-line, externality,* and *gross national product* replace the classical concerns of service, matching goods with needs, social commerce, and home economics—has begun to cost us daily.

Examples of this forgetfulness abound. The editors of the magazine *Good Money* recently showed that the five corporations cited by Environmental Action for their neglectful environmental records—Weyerhauser, Occidental Petroleum, Standard Oil of Ohio (now AMOCO), Republic Steel, and Dow Chemical—were soundly and convincingly outperformed by five comparable companies with much better environmental records.

In contrast, ethical-based investors are demonstrating the long-standing common sense of betting on firms that keep the classical connections intact. The amount U.S. citizens have invested in socially screened funds has grown from $40 billion in 1984 to over $450 billion in 1989. Meanwhile, the Calvert Social Investment Fund earned thirty-three percent in 1986, while the market average for mutual funds was twenty-eight percent. Calvert, by August of 1989, handled $260 million for nearly thirty thousand investors.

Why is it, then, that films such as *Wall Street* continue to celebrate short-term greed, and publications like *Business Week* can cover the Economic Summit of 1989 without any serious accounting of its environmental content? Our answer is forgetfulness, a kind of capitalism so advanced in aggressiveness that it functions in a fashion more appropriately termed "senile" than "sensible."

For further reading on the subject, see the books of Allen Kneese, Kenneth Boulding, and Herman Daley. These three economists have explored, with tact and insight, the intricate debate about how we might evolve capitalist economies so as to refine and redirect our patterns of resource use. While other "radical" economists such as John Ruskin (1819–1900) and Richard Tawney (1880–1962) had broken ranks with the endlessly expanding "growth tradition" of modern economic theory, these three are those whose voices we've heard most incisively since World War II.

In 1966, in his now famous essay "The Spaceship Earth," Boulding defines our current economy as a "cowboy economy," where, "symbolic of the illimitable plains and also associated with reckless exploitative, romantic and violent behavior," people consume as if they lived in an endlessly open society. In its place, Boulding recommended "a spaceship economy" where "the essential measure of success . . . is not production and consumption at all, but the nature, extent, quality and complexity of the total capital stock, including in this state the state of the human bodies and minds included in the system." While Bruce Piasecki was still a student at Cornell, Boulding gave a brilliant set of lectures—aptly entitled "The Laws of Practically Everything"—where he explained quite convincingly why "grow-mania" economists emphasize income-flow concepts like "thruput" at the expense of the more reliable social measurement of "capital-stock" concepts.

Herman Daley's books, especially his *Economic, Ecology, Ethics: Essays Toward a Steady-State Economy,* go far in attempting to recouple ecology and economists. As a writer, Daley is at home with both cleverly conceived verbal distinctions and empirically based observations. A quick example, from his introduction to the title mentioned above, captures this insightful facility. Noting that the major cause of our environmental crisis is the fact that "the moral science of political economy has degenerated into the amoral game of political economics," Daley reminds us that in its origins "political economy" was concerned with scarcity. "Political economics," on the other hand, "attempts to buy off social conflict by abolishing scarcity—by promising more things for more people with less for no one, for ever and ever." Daley also has answers. Many of his works explore how "transferable birth rights" and "a system of depletion quotas," auctioned by government, can set us on a path he calls "steady-state economics," whereby the modern world need not be forgetful of the ecology-economy link.

Finally, Allen Kneese is our long-needed numbers cruncher, the exacting economist who documents the fundamental insanity of environmental abuse. After my first book, *Beyond Dumping*, came out in 1984, I was fortunate enough to see Kneese's review in *Natural Resources Journal*. His insightful comments mixed praise with a suggestion that caused me to write a second book on the issue of hazardous-waste management. When I brought *America's Future* to Kneese's office at Resources for the Future in Washington, D.C., I was impressed again by the stacks of data he has amassed to make his many points. For a volcanic source of information on the irrepressible common sense of environmental economics, please see Kneese's many books and articles.

Of course, libraries are full of other insightful critiques of "senile" capitalism, such as those by E. F. Schumacher, Nicholas Georgeseu-Roegen, Lester Brown, and Garrett Hardin. But if you wish to get wholesome and readable commentary, Boulding, Hardin, and Kneese are recommended first.

CHAPTER 2

1. Naomi Shohno, *The Legacy of Hiroshima* (Tokyo: Kosei Publishing Co., 1986).
2. On July 31, 1989, Keith Schneider reported in *The New York Times* that the first wave of cleanups will address ninety-four separate sites in nineteen different states, of which seventy-two are no longer active. These are the sites already acknowledged by DOE.

    When we say there are eight hundred contaminated sites, this is as defined by law, not as defined by function or facility. There are, as our map shows, several distinct facilities in the identified nineteen states. Yet the definitions of the federal Resource Conservation and Recovery Act and the hazardous-waste laws have already identified eighty-one different sites for remediation at Hanford alone. So if you hear officials speak about tens of facilities, or hundreds of different weapons-development functions, or thousands of contaminated sites, they are all right. The risks are the same; the variety comes in the terms experts come up with to describe the size of the problem.

3. Early in 1989, Glenn was instrumental in getting an additional $360 million from the Bush administration to help get cleanup planning underway in 1990. Over the long haul our nation is going to have to come up with, according to Glenn, about $8 to $10 billion a year for the next thirty years. As time moves on, the budget battles over this issue will create a new brotherhood of cleanup companies that will continue to tax our economy.

    Energy Secretary James D. Watkins revealed that the Bush administration is committed to spending $21.5 billion over the course of the first part of the 1990s to repair the damage at ninety-four nuclear sites. In a letter sent to Congress on July 31, 1989, Watkins asserted the plan "is a major initiative in an effort to restore public credibility in the department's ability to operate safely its unique defense, research and test facilities." More skeptical analysts, including environmental groups, say the critical issue is the ratio of funding afforded to continue production of nuclear weapons versus the cleanup effort and on-going health and safety programs. "The trick," notes a Glenn aid, "is to force the right ratio between production and restoration."

4. This "mixed-waste" controversy was properly stopped by a 1987 court case filed by the Natural Resources Defense Council, and the Legal Environmental

Assistance Foundation against the Department of Energy. Gary Davis, co-author with Piasecki of *America's Future in Hazardous Waste Management,* was the lead attorney in the case that brought the federal facilities back into compliance with the same laws on toxics that commercial firms must obey.

5. Department of Energy: *Environment, Safety and Health Report for the DOE Defense Complex,* U.S. Printing Office: Washington, D.C., July 1, 1988, p. 34.

6. Much of this information is derived from Thomas B. Cochran's *U.S. Nuclear Warhead Facility Profiles* (vol. 3, 1987, pp. 15–18), as are the following details:

   Eight old retired graphite reactors sit with the controversial N-reactor in one section of the reservation. The fuel-processing and waste-storage areas take up roughly twice that area. Plans call for construction of the Hanford vitrification plant (the HWVP) beginning around 1990 in this storage zone. The fast-flux test facility, a 400-megawatt sodium-cooled fast reactor for testing fuels and materials for America's breeder reactor programs, is another major facility on the reservation, occupying another part of the complex quite far from the old retired reactors. Finally, another chunk of the reservation is devoted to fuel fabrication and R & D labs.

7. For a vivid account of that secrecy, see *Disaster in the Urals,* which describes a nuclear mishap striking an area the size of Pennsylvania.

8. We heard this tale of Mormon sales from multiple sources, one a defense contract administrator, another a resident of Richmond, Va., the third a resident of Seattle. In each case, the individual has reasons to remain unnamed. Thus, we print the paragraph without reference or details.

9. The fact that the federal government exempts its contractors in this risky business puts Americans in a condition of "double jeopardy." We suffer the risk of not knowing who's liable as we suffer the health risks themselves.

10. Westinghouse Electric Corp. benefited from a surge in power-plant equipment orders in the second quarter of 1989, according to the July 14, 1989, edition of *The Wall Street Journal.* Company profits increased from $215.3 million to $228.3 million in a one-year period. Company officials report that operating profits rose eleven percent during a time of a sluggish economy. Ironically, one of the prime forces behind this economic good news for Westinghouse is that three of four orders totaling $500 million in the first half of 1989 were for combined-cycle cogeneration plants, devices which more efficiently utilize fossil fuels and which are displacing utilities' previous nuclear-plant orders.

11. The figures on exposure from the Feeds Materials Production Center are obtained from the February 24, 1989, Radioactive Waste Campaign document entitled *Uranium Releases at Fernald: Radiation Doses to Nearby Residents.* R.W.C. is based in New York City.

12. These facts were derived from personal interviews and the transcripts of an April 28, 1987, hearing by the House Subcommittee on Oversight and Investigations, entitled *Environmental Compliance by Federal Agencies* (serial no. 100-39), pp. 97–99.

13. Carl Johnson, "Deadly Fallout from Rocky Flats Weapons Plant," *Sacramento Bee,* December 20, 1988, p. B9.

14. Such approaches to management are apparently a thing of the past. Energy Secretary James Watkins has been outspoken about how the separate culture operating at our weapons-complex sites was a result of too much emphasis on production at the expense of safety and the environment. In July 1989, he announced that at least fifty-one percent of performance awards paid to defense contractors would be based on compliance with federal and state environment, safety, and health regulations. In the past, said Watkins, about twenty percent of the awards related to such compliance.

15. What is astonishing about GAO's fifty reports on the weapons complex is the years of silence that accompanied their release. Since the 1970s, the GAO has been alerting Congress, in documents available to the public, that a huge cleanup bill and some horrendous health issues were looming.

16. OMB officials note that the funding for DOE "more than doubled during the Reagan years in percentage terms and funding for the environmental component increased much more dramatically." According to DOE figures, since 1985, the environmental, safety, and health budget has increased sixty percent for programs and fifty percent for staff. In 1988, a thirteen-percent budget increase went into effect, as did a ten-percent staff increase.

Perhaps the severity of the problem has been overstated, says OMB, questioning the true price tag on the cleanup. "We haven't had the time or the capability to look at cost estimates and see how realistic they are. There's been no scrubbing of these costs," said Joe Hezir, who oversees the budgets for all environmental, safety, and health programs.

Hezir admits that one shortcoming to the federal government's response to the nuclear-weapons production cleanup dilemma so far is that no support is being given to new innovative technological solutions. "That kind of thinking is just not going on right now," he remarked. Noting that no matter how much the figures are scrubbed, the price tags for cleanup promises to be enormous. Hezir acknowledged that the amount of money OMB is going to commit "is going to be a lot less than a lot of people would like to see."

17. America's most dangerous weapons-production waste, as well as accumulating wastes from U.S. commercial nuclear reactors, were to be stored at Yucca Mountain, 110 miles west of Las Vegas. This site lies between aerial bombardment and nuclear bomb-testing ranges and was selected in spite of warnings from DOE scientist Jerry Szymanski that it was "unsuitable" for permanent storage of nuclear waste. This is where the nuclear glass from Savannah will be shipped to. Nevada state officials report a laundry list of noncompliance with federal laws at Yucca, resulting in a loss of radioactive materials into nearby wells.

Ironically, when visiting Soviet scientists were monitoring nuclear testing at the contiguous nuclear testing range, they asserted that it would be naïve to think that nuclear testing would not contaminate local groundwater. The day after the assertion, DOE officials declared that such contamination was not possible.

The exempting of the siting of the Yucca facility from the traditional environmental impact statement mandated under the National Environmental Policy Act (NEPA), as well as from other standard siting procedures, calls into question the evolving process whereby the U.S. government will handle environmental reviews for complex, controversial projects in the future. According to Charles Malone, an environmental scientist for Nevada State who monitors federal efforts at Yucca, the weakening of NEPA by exemptions embodied in the Nuclear Waste Policy Amendments Act of 1987 is a trend that needs to be further scrutinized. Malone, in an article published in *Environmental Impact Assessment Review* in September 1989, concludes that it appears that "political expediency is more important to policy makers than environmental rationality. NEPA's procedural foundation was set aside and subsequently replaced by flawed practices that clearly fail to assure adequate protection of the environment."

Concerns about safety have also postponed the opening of the Waste Isolation Pilot Project in Carlsbad, New Mexico, where all of the nation's plutonium wastes will be processed and buried, and where, so the theory goes, the creep of local salt beds will close over the drums of waste. DOE's own engineers were not satisfied with the adequacy of this $700 million facility. It is expected to be opened in the early 1990s.

18. No matter what one's opinion of nuclear power's merits, if America is going to pursue further research and development with various forms of new, smaller, safer nuclear units, then this decision needs to be made within the context of a full range of affordable investments. While it is true that nuclear power does not contribute directly to greenhouse gases, the technology still has a tremendous problem of waste disposal. Furthermore, the costs of competing alternatives, such as solar and wind energy, are coming down, whereas nuclear's projections and costs seem to be heading in the opposite direction.

John W. Gofman, former director of the biomedical division of the Lawrence Livermore Laboratory and professor emeritus of Medical Physics at the University of California–Berkeley, claims that new interest in the nuclear option is misguided because nuclear power also contributes to global warming. According to Gofman, nuclear power adds to the heat of the earth's surface by liberating energy which otherwise would remain unfissioned in uranium and plutonium nuclei. "It's even possible that nuclear power will make a net addition to the greenhouse effect," states Gofman, "to the extent that large quantities of fossil fuels are burned in order to mine and refine the necessary uranium, to construct nuclear plants, to clean up their multimillion-dollar messes, and later to decommission them and put their deadly wastes somewhere. Given the poor performance of our nuclear plants so far, it is an open question whether they will end up producing any more net energy here than the fossil fuels consumed by them." Gofman says that energy efficiency and solar power, and a shakeup in the environmental movement, are the solutions to global warming and acid rain and the key for manufacturing reform.

If America is willing to gamble on the nuclear option, it must improve upon its past record, according to Peter Johnson, former administrator of the Bonneville Power Administration and a public official who was burned in effigy when he ordered the closing of two nuclear reactors in the infamous WHOOPS episode in the Pacific Northwest. WHOOPS, a play on WPPSS, an acronym for Washington Public Power Supply Systems, refers to immense cost overruns associated with nuclear plant construction that resulted in the largest bond default in United States history. Bringing a private-sector savvy to his job, Johnson blames much of the waste of research dollars in the nuclear area on a failure to base governmental decisions on facts verified by expert, disinterested third parties. "The contractors who run nuclear facilities have vested interests and different agendas than the public," noted Johnson; because government oversight is so unfocused, programs move forward with their own misguided momentums.

"The past approach to nuclear research and development has been a chaotic, self-serving disaster," claims Johnson, who encourages future efforts to design a "truly open-minded and directed process-oriented methodology based on due process." Strict tests of efficiency have to be included to weed out pork-barrel politics, and the public needs to be brought into the debate so that the information flow to decision-makers is not limited to "just the major stakeholders," such as those receiving lucrative operation contracts.

John F. Ahearne, a former Nuclear Regulatory Commission official and current senior fellow at Resources for the Future, offers a modest start to try to regain confidence in the nuclear power industry. He recommends that higher standards of crew competence be mandatory; that weak utilities transfer control to operating companies; and that renewals of operating licenses be required every five years. He also suggests that to break the trend of plant manufacturers utilizing a series of subcontractors, new nuclear regulations should "require each manufacturer work with only one company in the design of the non-reactor part of the power plant." He proposes that Congress legislate standardized plants and more streamlined licensing procedures, too.

Whether we as a nation move forward with nuclear power will be a critical test of how we define affordability. Given the immense challenge facing us concerning our past mistakes managing the nuclear-weapons production complex, are we prepared to continue to rely on nature's resilience when the answers to the radioactive-waste problem are still mired in controversy? We can't afford to ignore government's role in stimulating environmentally sound innovations in energy production. Faced with tough choices, should government expand nuclear power research and development, when our competition is threatening us with a range of other alternatives?

Look around the world, and it becomes evident what others view as affordable. In the wind-power arena, the Dutch have doubled the U.S. request for research funding ($19 million compared to $8.3 million for 1990). India is planning to spend $25.6 million on wave power, an item not even in the U.S. budget. And the United Kingdom has doubled our investment in geothermal power ($6.21 million compared to $3.5 million).

19. "Decommissioning is a beast," said a New York State Energy Research and Development official leading a charge to find new ways to "cleanse the old babies" without immense radioactive-waste generation. The early examples and estimates from Three Mile Island and Shoreham do not look cheap, easy, or particularly safe to workers or residents. Some of the proposed decommissioning techniques are simply too primitive. Sandblasting the walls of reactors, for instance, leaves quite a volume of contaminated sand.

20. Three reports from the GAO document the similar challenges facing the nuclear-weapons complex and commercial nuclear power industry: *NRC's Decommissioning Cost Estimates Appear Low* (GAO/RCED-88-184), July 1988; *What Can Be Done to Revive the Nuclear Option?* (GAO/RCED-89-67), March 1989; *NRC's Decommissioning Procedures and Criteria Need to Be Strengthened* (GAO/RCED-89-119), May 1989.

21. Asmus covered the campaigns surrounding Rancho Seco very closely for McGraw-Hill's *Electric Utility Week* as well as for *California Energy Markets*, two well-respected trade newsletters. Here is a brief summary of the campaign:

A citizen's group, Sacramentans for SAFE Energy, placed a Rancho Seco shutdown initiative, Measure B, on the June 1988 ballot. The SMUD board, dominated by a cast of characters that might get Rod Serling out of his grave for one more *Twilight Zone*, then drafted its own ballot initiative, Measure C, which would have given "the Ranch" an eighteen-month-trial operation period.

The measure to close Rancho Seco failed by less than one percentage point. The measure to keep it open passed on a close vote. Part of Measure C stipulated a second election. This was scheduled less than eighteen months after the first balloting to ensure that the municipal utility district would avoid the expensive refueling process if voters voted to shut the plant down. SMUD's general manager, who had recommended that the utility close the plant, was fired shortly after the election, and the head of Rancho Seco nuclear operations resigned as the board announced yet another set of rate increases due to Seco repairs. A SMUD board election in November 1988 resulted in three new board members: one aligned with the pronuclear lobby and two affiliated with democratic ratepayer groups. Incumbent Ed Semloff, a consistent Seco foe, appeared to be the heir apparent to the board presidency, but newcomer Joe Buonaiuto got the support of the two pronuclear members to become president. Though Buonaiuto was elected as a ratepayer advocate highly skeptical of Rancho Seco, he soon became its most rabid advocate.

During the first election, Rancho Seco employees produced massive quantities of signs, buttons, and even T-shirts. They filled meeting after meeting of the SMUD board and booed and hissed anyone who dared doubt the reactor's ability to deliver. The opposition, which included Santa Monica Assemblyman Tom Hayden's Campaign California, was vastly outspent and seemed unprepared for the almost ferocious tactics of plant employees and other plant supporters. When presidential candidate Jesse Jackson made a trip out to "the Ranch" he was heckled so relentlessly that he broke off the news conference.

In the second election, those opposed to Rancho Seco became worried about their "fringe" antinuclear image, and groomed a middle-of-the-road message to highlight that it was the kooks who wanted to keep the plant open. Those in favor of Rancho Seco, stung by the free publicity those opposed to Seco had achieved in the 1988 election because of the fairness doctrine, avoided the airwaves and instead relied on a massive signposting and door-to-door campaign.

Measure K, favoring the plant, was defeated in June 1989. Talk of converting the reactor to run on natural gas—as well as a solar thermal technology—then followed, and serves as a preview of the types of proposals that will reappear with increasing frequency during the 1990s as the nation tries to cull what it can from a nuclear industry in transition.

22. It is highly ironic that Bush, a Republican, has pushed so hard for Shoreham. Republican instincts center around notions of local control and entrepreneurship; in this case, however, Bush's position ignores the facts that local officials have spoken against the plant, and that nuclear power has repeatedly flunked the test of the marketplace.

23. The Swedish nuclear program has been a model of efficiency: its twelve reactors operate at eighty-four percent of maximum capacity.

CHAPTER 3

1. It is too early to gain any firm factual hold on the changes now called global warming, since most of these changes, even the experts admit, may never be fully known in advance. Four factors—clouds, oceans, solar cycles, and volcanoes—may serve to illustrate the remarkable complexity of global warming. "Clouds," admits expert V. Ramanathan of the University of Chicago, "are one of the largest sources of uncertainty." A warmer earth should mean more humidity, and thereby more clouds. But it is also thought that clouds could cool things off by increasing the reflection of solar energy. So it is hard to predict which effect might dominate a cloudier world.

Oceans are massive heat absorbers, but just how long they can delay the full onset of global warming is still hotly debated. Volcanoes cool the earth's overall surface, but no one can predict when the big ones will erupt. And solar cycles show that, while many believe the sun's output is constant, it's not. Brightness, for instance, diminished about 0.1 percent from 1979 to 1984.

How clouds, oceans, volcanoes, and sun cycles interact is still an untold story, more like a Brahms symphony than a science.

Most experts agree, however, that the policies being pursued to combat global warming—the saving of the rain forest, greater energy efficiency, and less fossil-fuel use—are useful and needed policy initiatives regardless of whether the world is cooling or warming. These policies should be viewed as an insurance policy for future generations.

2. The record heat of 1988 simply replaced the previous record set in 1987. The years 1981 and 1983 tied for third-warmest, with 1980 and 1986 in fifth and six places, respectively. These records hold for all recorded weathers in history.

3. "The combined atmospheric buildup of carbon dioxide and other greenhouse gases since 1860," notes Irving M. Mintzer of the World Resources Institute, "are believed to have already committed the earth's surface to warm approximately 0.5° to 1.5°C. above the average global temperature of the pre-industrial period." This doesn't sound like much, but actually represents an astonishing amount of released heat. A change in average global temperature of only 1°C. separates today's climate regime from that of the "little ice age" period of the thirteenth through seventeenth centuries in Europe and North America. So the increase of 2.1° to 8.1°F. (which is 1.5° to 4.5°C.) represents a massive increase atop the already noted changes.

4. These round figures come from research performed by Skidaway Institute of Oceanography for a position paper entitled *Saving the American Beach,* presented by the Concerned Coastal Geologists at Savannah, Georgia, in 1981. These figures, therefore, understate the extent of the damage. Orrin H. Pilkey, Jr., of Duke University, along with William J. Neal of Grand Valley State College, have edited a series of reports sponsored by the National Audubon Society, entitled *Living with the Shore.* This series goes into great detail on the numerous restoration projects now underway on all American coastlines.

5. U.S. Environmental Protection Agency, *The Potential Effects of Global Climate Change on the United States,* draft report (vol. 2), Oct. 1988, pp. 12–14.

6. Getting off the petrochemical treadmill means a sustained and concentrated effort—a process of withdrawal, not a drunk man's dive. The change will not happen overnight. As California's efforts show, the trick is increasing the use of alternatives to fossil fuels. The state was once dependent upon fossil fuels for about eighty percent of its energy needs, but that percentage has almost been sliced in half, as safer substitutes have been found for about a third of the state's energy needs.

   For more specific and technically detailed information about California and other states' efforts, see "State Energy Policies and Global Warming," by Peter Asmus and Bruce Piasecki, *California Policy Choices* (vol. 5) (Sacramento, Calif.: University of Southern California School of Public Administration, 1989).

7. Despite our characterization of Exxon and other multi-national oil companies as preoccupied with a fossil-fuel future, the world's biggest oil company—Royal Dutch Shell—is a model of long-range planning, with a growing emphasis on incorporating environmental concerns into the picture. Royal Dutch Shell was the first to push unleaded gas and is experimenting with greater use of less polluting natural gas.

   Unlike many of the oil companies who abandoned solar development in the 1980s, Mobil is still aggressively researching the use of photovoltaics for future utility use. At present, the firm produces the largest, most powerful flat-plate module in the world. Despite its finely honed green image, however, environmentalists have criticized the company for its involvement with an aluminum smelter and bauxite mine in the Amazon rain forest.

8. Claudine Schneider, "Least-Cost Utility Planning: Providing a Competitive Edge," *Public Utilities Fortnightly,* Apr. 17, 1986, p. 15.

9. In *The Control of Oil* (New York: Vintage Books, 1976), John Blair argues that institutional barriers are the prime impediment preventing us from ending our

almost sentimental love of oil. His prescription is to sever the cozy relationships between regulator and regulated. He calls for the vigorous enforcement of antitrust laws to allow market forces to break up the big oil companies and to shape public policy. An end to depletion allowances and tax breaks would do the same.

His view, from over a decade ago, still rings with some truth: "In mutual dislike, rather than in mutual understanding, there is strength. Moreover, by making an industry's behavior depend on the judgment and actions of many buyers and sellers, the competitive approach minimizes the harm that can be done by any small groups of individuals, thereby making influence and corruption more cumbersome, expensive, and of most importance, ineffective."

The new concerns about greenhouse gases, however, change the agenda for the oil lobby, and require a quicker resolution than Blair's "mutual dislike." No matter how entrenched the petrochemical treadmill may be in society, the more efficient use of fossil fuels will be mandated by political reality. This is the first step to be taken in response to environmental concerns, because it is the easiest and most cost-effective.

10. Robert Heilbroner, *An Inquiry into the Human Prospect,* 3rd ed. (New York: W. W. Norton, 1980), p. 43.

11. Two articles, appearing in the Mar. 17, 1989, *Christian Science Monitor,* highlight the market opportunities that will open up because of retrofits required by acid rain: Richard Wentworth, "Cost and Profit in Cutting Acid Rain," and John Borley, "Canadian Smelter to Spend $500 Million to Cut Emissions," both on p. 9.

12. See the Electric Power Research Institute's *Global Climate Change and the Electric Power Industry* (presented at the Jan. 5, 1988, National Climate Program Office's Strategic Planning Seminar), pp. 8–13.

13. An example of "unneeded" high-tech investments of government research dollars is the Tokomak project at Princeton University. This project studies the principles of magnetic fusion to create little stars on earth. At best, the commercial application of superconducting magnets to create some glow in every basement is decades off. Lavishly funded research projects such as Tokomak are full-employment acts for academia's brightest and best. But we must resist, at times, chasing esoteric dreams and developing research toys that may never leave the laboratory. If Tokomak received only twenty percent less funding, thousands of homes could be made more energy-efficient for seventy years. The choice is tough. Obviously, big science cannot be the only path of reform.

14. An example of a "damaging" use of federal research dollars is our large investments in enhanced oil-recovery techniques, since their success only keeps us on the petrochemical treadmill. Back in 1905, America's discovery of abundant oil at Spindletop made its extraction simple and cost-effective. After World War II, the nation's emphasis shifted to "secondary" oil recovery, whereby steam helped isolate remnant oil in known reserve areas. At present, enhanced or "tertiary" oil recovery entails going back to spent oil-recovery sites and, through the use of surfactants that wash out oil like soap removes grease from dishes, removing the last drips. After this oil is pumped up using steam pressure, another process separates usable oil from surfactants. Some critics, like E. F. Schumacher, claim that the resultant unit of energy is less than the energy consumed to produce, pump, and refine it for commercial applications. In short, another treadmill.

15. See William Chandler, "Views of OECD, The Soviet Union and China." Chandler, a senior scientist for Battelle Memorial Institute, Pacific Northwest Laboratories, prepared this study for submission to the University of California–Davis Panel on Prospects for International Action on Global Climate Change,

Sept. 6, 1989. He points out that the most effective method to combat global warming may be to set specified energy-efficient improvement rates, or establish goals for carbon dioxide–release reductions based on a nation's gross national product per-unit ratios. This would be a positive way to go about achieving reforms, since these measures would be perceived as being fair to everybody as they would increase rather than retard economic development.

16. Walt Whitman was one of a number of writers on both sides of the Atlantic who advocated extreme reshaping of the environment during the second half of the nineteenth century. His works present "a new race dominating previous ones," which should, in time, inhabit the entire globe and transform nature into "a new earth." He celebrated his century's great changes—the proliferation of rail-roads, steamships, cotton gins, and telegraph lines in "Passage to India," and the felling of California's redwoods in "Song of the Redwood Tree"—as symbols of an irresistible and impending succession to a "new earth," and as icons of a longing in modern man for complete transformation of the environment.

17. The banking policies of the World Bank affect two-thirds of the world's ecological wonders. Typical of the misguided sort of project that the bank has funded in the past is a recent proposal to loan Brazil over $1 billion for huge hydroelectric projects that would flood hundreds of miles of dense tropical rain forests and displace another population of indigenous people. The bank has been urged by environmentalists to turn to smaller-scale projects that allow the existing human, animal and plant natives some dignity. Instead of monster dams to produce electricity that may never be needed, the banks should promote a range of environmentally benign energy alternatives such as simple solar heat pumps.

Progress was beginning to show in Brazil in 1988. Ironically, economic difficulties, which have hampered environmental protection, are reducing damaging public-works projects as well. Utilities in Brazil are now trying to factor in environmental costs in their decisions, at least temporarily stalling previously planned dams. On top of that, a broad policy initiative entitled Nossa Natureza ("Our Nature") has obtained the support of the country's military and is coordinating the activities of Brazil's four environmental-protection bodies.

Perhaps the most promising tool to save rain forests is debt-for-nature swaps. Such swaps involve the purchase of a developing country's debt at a discounted value in the secondary market, and cancellation of that debt in return for environment-related action on the part of the debtor nation. Such swaps have already occurred, or are being contemplated, in Brazil, Bolivia, Costa Rica, Ecuador, Chile, Mexico, Argentina, and the Philippines.

18. The required retrofits would cost $300 million to $500 million, yet they would also reduce the trade deficit by $20 billion to $40 billion annually because of the ability to reduce oil imports by 2 million to 3.5 million barrels per day.

LBL proposes a number of innovative policies to accomplish these goals. One of the more fascinating is a "gas guzzler/sipper fee/rebate program" for automobiles. This revenue neutral fee/rebate scheme would propose a fee on new cars based on their fuel efficiency. Efficient cars such as the Honda Civic American would receive, based on 1987 calculations, a rebate of $1,250, whereas gas guzzlers like the Ferrari Testarossa would pay large fees. During a transition phase, the rebates would be paid in proportion to American-made content and labor, in order not to alienate the American auto manufacturers, allowing them to gradually shift production away from the less efficient cars that currently dominate their sales. Additional registration fee incentives, along with a modest ten-cents-per-year gas tax, would, according to LBL's Rosenfeld, allow the marketplace to promote better efficiency without severe economic dislocation.

Other proposals include sliding-scale hookup fees and rebates for new commercial and residential buildings, and developing a carbon dioxide tax for all fifty states, with rebates given to those utilities who shift away from the petrochemical treadmill fastest. It is these kinds of specific adjustments, once freed from this age of environmental blame, that will bring substantive reforms into the world.

19. It is ironic, considering how closely allied DOE is with oil interests, that their own reports encourage getting off the petrochemical treadmill. DOE has drawn most of its leaders, appointed by the president, from among oil people. It wasn't until the Hanford and Savannah problems described in Chapter 2 became so large that James Watkins, an ex-nuclear navy official, became the first secretary of energy with a background outside the oil industry.

20. New York's efforts are impressive, but in the Soviet Union, seventy percent of residential users participate in district heating and cooling programs, while the U.S. overall percentage is infinitesimal. Nevertheless, much of this coordination in the Soviet Union is wasted because of a lack of temperature controls. The most common method of interior temperature control is opening windows, even in winter.

21. Another emerging trend is the notion of "hard solar," whereby huge photovoltaic farms would be stationed in the Southwest to generate electricity for different parts of the nation. The problem with solar energy has always been finding enough insolation in enough parts of the country to enable widespread applications, and the ability to store the energy, once it has been created, for use when the sun is down. However, when the energy produced by photovoltaics is converted into liquid hydrogen fuel, it could theoretically be stored and transported to less sunny parts of the country for use. With certain policy changes, researchers such as Robert Williams of Princeton predict, such technological breakthroughs could occur as early as the beginning of the next century.

It is projected that thirty to forty percent of New Mexico would need to be utilized in order to displace current fossil-fuel consumption. From an international perspective, it would take 1.7 percent of the land mass of our deserts, or 3.6 percent of the world's agricultural land, to displace world fossil-fuel use.

22. These statistics, as well as others scattered throughout this chapter, were presented by Claudine Schneider, Republican Representative from Rhode Island, in an article entitled "Preventing Climatic Change," in the Summer 1989 edition of *Issues in Science and Technology*. Schneider writes: "The slow pace of climate change breeds complacency, but we must remember that the climate will also be slow to respond to after-the-fact solutions. We must begin now to adopt the good stewardship practices that will reduce the likelihood of human-induced climate disruption." She also notes: "A fifty percent cut since 1980 in the federal energy efficiency R&D budget has meant that there have been no new research projects begun this decade. These budget cuts seem particularly shortsighted in light of the spectacular success of federal energy-efficiency R&D. According to a 1987 analysis by the American Council for an Energy Efficient Economy, the $16 million that DOE spent on cooperative projects with industry to develop heat pumps, more efficient refrigerators, new ballasts to improve the efficiency of fluorescent lights, and glass coatings that control heat loss and gain through windows will help save the country billions of dollars through energy savings."

23. There is a ray of hope from Texas in the form of an ambitious $100 million building retrofit program, most of it earmarked for state-owned institutions. This program is funded, appropriately enough, by Exxon funds obtained by way of a settlement regarding petroleum price-control violations between 1973 and 1981. Texas owns more state buildings than any other state, and therefore

is the perfect testing ground for such new conservation technologies. The most promising aspect of the program, however, is that the program will institutionalize a series of incentives—in the form of savings and bonuses—for new energy-audit managers to exceed efficiency targets. The eight-year program began in July 1988. It will provide a critical data base from which the nation can shape a national strategy.

24. Much of the information from Robert Williams is included in a paper entitled: "Biomass Gasifier/Gas Turbine Power and the Greenhouse Warming," and was presented at the International Energy Administration/Organization for Economic Competition and Development Seminar on Energy Technologies for Reducing Emissions of Greenhouse Gases in April 1989 in Paris. For more information, contact Director, Center for Energy and Environmental Studies, Princeton University, Princeton, NJ 08544.

25. Tax credits and long-term, fixed-price contracts have been maligned by critics, but they provided important help to the infant renewable-energy industry. Tax credits, which were repealed at the end of 1988, eventually became unpopular because some opportunists abused bogus wind and solar projects for tax-credit write-off purposes.

   Even more valuable as a helping hand to LUZ and other independent power producers were California's Standard Offer 4 contracts. These contracts, developed by the California Public Utilities Commission, were initially based on projected prices for future oil. Averaging about seven cents per kilowatt-hour, some contracts extended fifteen to thirty years. These contracts attracted much-needed financing for innovative solar, wind, and geothermal projects.

   An unexpected large response from applicants, coupled with the rapid fall in oil prices, led to the suspension of SO 4 contracts in April 1985. Numerous "paper projects"—projects which may never exist in reality—contracts were approved before the SO 4 deadline, and forecasting how many of these will actually come on-line has become a convoluted shell game that has, unfortunately, undermined the credibility of renewable energy resources.

   In 1989, the California Legislature reinstated a solar tax credit, but limited it to electricity generating systems. This is yet another example of how governments are realizing the benefits of innovation.

CHAPTER 4

1. President Jimmy Carter, in the 1970s, initiated the idea of residential energy-efficient home mortgages, but this effort foundered due to a lack of paperwork consistency among the five federal agencies that offer energy-efficiency mortgages. This lack of consistency, when coupled with a lack of a standardized method of rating the economic value of energy conservation improvements, has deterred widespread adoption of even limited energy-efficiency upgrades.

2. An exact replica of the Swedish example would be difficult for the United States because of the fragmented nature of our housing industry. Yet a Lawrence Livermore Laboratory study outlines where we have gone wrong and offers some tips for homeowners. Entitled *Planning for an Energy-Efficient Tomorrow*, the report points out that to date, most U.S. programs were hodgepodge promotions easily implemented. Financial incentives are not enough, states this report, noting that participation is dependent upon training, education, and technical assistance. The writers cite as a cause for optimism statistics showing that, when participating in "home energy rating system" programs, homeowners reduced energy bills by thirty to fifty percent. The bottom line of the report is that a long-term, comprehensive perspective is needed in order to stimulate

the various players—builders, mortgage lenders, real estate agents—into participating in these programs.

Among the many sensible reforms proposed in the report is a streamlining of the so-called energy-efficient home mortgage to roll the cost of energy improvements into the mortgage. Under such a plan, the amount of money saved by the energy improvements would be quantified and used as qualifying income for buyers, thus making housing more affordable as well as more environmentally appropriate.

3. For a colorful account of the role utilities played in the growth and use of electrical appliances, see Martin Melosi's *Coping with Abundance* (New York: Random House, 1986).

4. The most effective way to reduce air pollution is to remove the source of the pollution. In the home, that may mean replacing a kerosene space heater with an electric one. Pesticides, termite controls, and herbicides should be removed from the house and stored in areas away from family living spaces. To reduce your exposure to nitrogen dioxide and carbon monoxide from your gas range, install an exhaust. You can also increase ventilation without giving up energy savings by installing an air-to-air heat exchanger. Such an exchanger captures ninety percent of the energy savings associated with house-tightening measures.

5. For more details about MCS and Dana Miller's plight, see the Winter 1988 volume of *Amicus Journal,* published by the Natural Resources Defense Council.

6. *Family, Work & Health Survey Report,* sponsored by the Commonwealth of Massachusetts, November 1988. Copies can be obtained by contacting the Women's Health Unit, Dept. of Public Health, 150 Tremont St., Boston, Mass. 02111

7. A sign of the times is a new magazine entitled simply *Garbage.* Dedicated to hands-on and practical tips about redesigning homes and lives to address growing environmental concerns, *Garbage* is but one publication that addresses the needs of a public in search of answers. Write to: *Garbage,* 435 Ninth St., Brooklyn, N.Y. 11215.

8. Ironically, the main feature that attracted industry to CFCs—their chemical stability—is also a curse. Even if use of CFCs were stopped instantaneously, the breakdown of ozone by CFCs already in the atmosphere would last for at least one hundred years.

The ozone story exemplifies how even if we have technology at our fingertips, our trust in the status quo can be intoxicating. After all, the now well-known Antarctic ozone hole began appearing as early as 1977, but went unreported for so long because scientists couldn't believe what their high-tech instruments were telling them. Then, in May 1985, a group of British scientists finally reported that for eight years in a row during September and October a mysterious loss of ozone had occurred. By 1984, the amount of ozone present was forty percent below what had been routinely reported some twenty years earlier.

9. Since the car remains the industrialized world's most sacred cow, it is hard to realize how long these machines have been milking us. History can add perspective, as these two quotes from the 1960s show. The first is from the great American historian Daniel J. Boorstin: "Seldom has a people found in technology so appropriate, so versatile, and so pervasive an expression. Originating in Europe, the automobile acquired novel forms in the United States. Although it remained a toy for the few in most of Europe, within a half century it had become a new social force touching everyone—an expression of and an instrument for speedy movement around and across the continent and up the social scale."

John B. Rae, in his 1965 book *The American Automobile,* develops this idea of the car as a social force, and its captivating link with upward mobility, as follows: "During its first three-quarters of a century, the American automobile had evolved into something much more than a conventional medium for getting from here to there. It is transportation, it is prestige, it is recreation. In one way or another, it supports one-sixth of all business enterprises and one-seventh of all wage earners. It has become almost indispensable as an adjunct to court-ship."

10. The fact that new kinds, not models, of cars are on the horizon represents a radical change. According to *The Future of the Automobile,* a collection of articles assembled by MIT, the basic idea of an automobile, and its many component parts, have remained essentially unaltered for a hundred years. This is remarkable in a world where building and bridge design, as well as machine parts, change almost annually. This is another example of the stagnating power of the petrochemical treadmill.

11. For more details on the costs of air pollution, please see *The Costs of Clean Air,* issued in July 1989 by the California Energy Commission.

12. While flexible-fuel cars running on methanol show great promise, researchers at the New York State Energy Research and Development Authority have taken a more cautious, skeptical approach, testing the actual emissions performance of these cars. Because the current generation of alternative-fuel cars can be finicky, New York is investigating whether tightening up inspection and maintenance requirements for traditionally fueled cars is yet another part of the answer.

Researchers are also retrofitting urban buses to see if a chemical additive can cut down on emissions. By 1991, tougher federal standards for urban bus emissions will force municipalities to switch from dirty diesel fuel, which compounds urban smog. Because an additive approach could be mobilized within a short time frame, such a move would have obvious benefits for Los Angeles as well.

Today, roughly half of all the oil consumed in America is used for transportation. The American Gas Association predicts that by the end of the century about half of the taxicabs, delivery trucks, and police cars will be running on natural gas. In Brooklyn, New York, two buses powered by compressed natural gas rather than diesel fuel give commuters a glimpse of the future.

Other alternative fuels include hydrogen, which can be derived from coal or natural gas and can be combined with oxygen to generate electricity. NASA currently utilizes hydrogen this way in our space program. A hydrogen-powered fuel-cell bus would offer dual air quality benefits since it would not emit any air pollution. On top of that, recent research by David Rind and cohorts for NASA's Goddard Institute for Space Studies implies that greenhouse gases will make weather systems more sluggish and increase the localized problems of urban smog. Since the hydrogen-powered vehicle would not contribute to the greenhouse effect, its use would bring additional benefits in the form of reducing the negative effect of emissions from conventional cars in industrial cities across the country.

13. This is how William Tucker, in his May 1979 cover story for *Harper's,* once highlighted our nation's former unfounded faith in American car manufacturers: "The myths once attached to the American Frontier have now been transferred to the American industrial system. They are vast reservoirs of wealth capable of absorbing any financial, psychological or social whim or fancy that people attach to them."

14. Already, the state of Vermont has banned the use of the single largest U.S. contributor car to ozone depletion: car air conditioners that use CFC-12, the

most damaging of CFCs. Since Vermont's average temperature for July is just 70 degrees, the measure is relatively painless. More important than the ban, nonetheless, is the effort by car manufacturers to find a substitute ingredient. At present, research is focusing on a chemical known as 134-A.

15. Among the challenges facing your backyard is human waste. We have already addressed the tragedy of disposable diapers. Your sewer system is part of yet another environmental quagmire. Once again, NASA's research provides a valuable spinoff. In this case, the tough task of wastewater treatment becomes a way to beautify an environment by planting floating water hyacinths.

   That's how the city of Haughton, Louisiana, complied with EPA wastewater standards. By creating an eleven-acre sewage lagoon with a seventy-by-nine-hundred-foot water hyacinth garden, the city is projected to be able to double its size while paying a third of the cost of typical technological upgrades required for such sewage growth. These savings are a result of the fact that water hyacinths thrive on sewage. After digestion by the water hyacinths, Haughton's sewage flows across a microbe-filled rock bed. Additional plants living in these rock beds then help deodorize the water. After the lagoon's first year of use, Haughton's sewer user fees were reduced by twenty-five percent.

CHAPTER 5

1. Information on benefits associated with new state-of-the-art electrical generation technologies developed in the United States comes from a study performed by the Oakland-based Independent Power Corporation (IPC), one of the nation's foremost energy analysis and forecasting firms. The study reveals that the nation's worst air in smoggy Los Angeles could be substantially improved through the introduction of new geothermal, wind, solar, and cogeneration technologies without any additional cost to ratepayers. By retiring half of its aging and polluting oil and gas power plants, and replacing these plants with the aforementioned mix of new, proven, commercially available technologies, Southern California Edison could cut its releases of nitrous oxide by sixty-five percent. (Nitrous oxide is a greenhouse gas that helps form ozone, an air pollutant that surpasses federal standards in Los Angeles two hundred days out of every year.)

   "Seven of the top twenty nitrous oxide polluters in the basin are power plants," points out consultant Michael Eaton. "Retiring 4,300 megawatt of Edison's plants would save ratepayers $1.5 billion and cut oil and gas consumption by fifty percent," he added. "It makes no sense to have ratepayers subsidize the continued operation of these old plants," adds IPC president Roy Alper.

   Part of the reason for these economic savings is that independent power producers cannot recoup overrun costs. They must absorb all of the environmental compliance costs, and only get paid when they produce power.

2. There is a glimmer of hope on the horizon for American investments in alternative sources of power, due in large part to the efforts of California Congressman Vic Fazio. Fazio not only secured funding for PVUSA, but he led the charge to increase federal research-and-development funding for 1990 from OMB's proposed thirty-percent cut to a net increase of over $36 million. Fazio, who has been perhaps the nation's most persistent supporter of solar power, was also instrumental in bringing to Fairfield, California, a photovoltaic manufacturing plant that includes among its investors Pacific Gas & Electric and labor-union pension funds.

3. Though Japan has become the envy of much of the world because of its indus-

trial prowess, the country has also attracted the wrath of environmentalists who complain about its ferocious pursuit of limited resources beyond its borders. Perhaps the most haunting image of Japan's disregard for the ecological balance necessary to preserve resources for future use is its forty-foot, fine-mesh fishing nets, often described as "walls of death." Australian scientists now fear that continued use of these nets will drive populations of albacore tuna into extinction. In addition, the nets entangle and needlessly kill great numbers of dolphins.

Japan has also been criticized for deforestation practices in Thailand and the Philippines, as well as Malaysia. The country has a history of harvesting endangered species to make jewelry—such as elephant ivory and hawksbill turtle shells. Environmental groups point out that Japan has failed to include these issues in their decision-making process regarding World Bank loan policies.

In response to international complaints, Japan has budgeted large sums of aid for developing nations. Also, Japanese conservationists, a rarity in a country dominated by an obsession with technology and competition, are becoming increasingly militant in their opposition to the large, destructive public-works projects commonly found throughout developing nations.

4. Washington, D.C.: Conservation Foundation, 1988.
5. New York: Basic Books, 1990.
6. H. Jeffrey Leonard, *Are Environmental Regulations Driving U.S. Industry Overseas?* (Washington, D.C.: Conservation Foundation, 1987).
7. *Project 88* was funded by the Carnegie Corporation of New York, the Richard King Mellon Foundation, the Rockefeller Family and Associates, and Keystone Center/Madison Associates.
8. After four years and $10 million in development costs, forty-two-year-old inventor Craig Linden, of the Alpine, California–based Microgen, Inc., is scaring utility bosses who fear his invention will put them out of business. In the past, cogeneration, the process of recapturing on-site waste heat, was primarily an industrial enterprise. But Linden's "micro" units, which range from 5 to 5,000 kilowatts, and which run quietly at approximately ninety-three-percent efficiency, can be installed in any home. The secret to his success is insulation, which captures otherwise wasted heat, resulting in more efficient start-ups, longer engine life, and fewer cold-start pollutants.

    Originally designed for combat use by the U.S. Navy, the system is the quietest on the market. With patents pending in twenty-two different countries, this discovery could transform the way our nation and others produce energy, forming a bridge to renewable energy technologies of the future. It also could put American inventors back in the limelight.
9. "Issues and Applications: Ohio Coal, or Environmental Compliance Made Costly," chapter 15 of *Managerial Economics and Public Policy*, pp. 565–69.
10. President Bush's new Clean Air Act is identifying the path to reform, by allowing utilities the flexibility to reduce sulfur dioxide emissions in the most cost-effective manner possible. The American Council for an Energy Efficient Economy (ACEEE) has identified several improvements to Bush's proposal that will allow utilities to reduce the anticipated costs of retrofitting old power plants by simply reducing the amount of energy consumed.

    According to the ACEEE, the anticipated billions of dollars in pollution-control equipment required in the nation's heartland—the sulfur-burning midwestern states such as Ohio—could be reduced by twenty-five percent or more if better efficiency were aggressively pursued. In order for this to occur, the

Clean Air Act regulations should set emission ceilings instead of rate limits, and allow utilities to count conservation investments as pollution cleanup for purposes of qualifying for federal subsidies.

11. Washington, D.C.: The Conservation Foundation, 1982.

12. The booming trade in exporting unwanted wastes to developing nations is one of the more frightening signs that a strict U.S. regulatory approach fails to recognize the international scope of the problem. Each year the number of waste shipments bound for countries such as Guatemala, the Philippines, or nearby Mexico has increased. Mexico is a particularly troublesome situation, as more than 1,300 *maquiladoras*, or "twin plants" that exist along the U.S.–Mexico border are pouring a noxious brew into waterways and deserts, some of it coming back to haunt U.S. citizens.

13. For elaborate examples and sustained evidence of this European approach, see Piasecki and Gary A. Davis, *America's Future in Hazardous Waste Management: Lessons from Europe* (Westport, Conn.: Greenwood Press, 1988).

14. E. F. Schumacher's classic book *Small Is Beautiful* (New York: Harper & Row, 1974) first offered this more affordable view some twenty years ago. His assistant, George McRobie, has built upon Schumacher's ideas with *Small Is Possible*, which outlines a reform agenda for transforming a world scarred by old, wasteful habits. "Conventional industrial societies are on a collision course with human nature, with the living environment, and the world's stock of nonrenewable resources," states McRobie. He warns that we cannot allow developing nations to repeat the same mistakes we have made.

Increased coal use by developing nations underlines McRobie's worries. These countries need small-scale renewable energy projects that match the needs of local citizens. McRobie remarks that through the use of "intermediate technologies" the United States and others "can help the helpless help themselves." For example, the industrialized world's preference to reduce labor needs is often at odds with developing nations' goals. "Tools and machines can be designed for micro-enterprises that are more productive than traditional technologies, and are low-cost and job-creating rather than labor displacing," notes McRobie.

15. It should be noted that Piasecki and Davis advised Dr. Bernard Fleet of Toronto as he built the TRSI system. Fleet had approached Piasecki about his new on-site approach after reading *Beyond Dumping*.

16. Gary Davis's forthcoming book tells the elaborate story of "safe substitutes." For offprints, contact Davis directly at the University of Tennessee's Waste Management Institute in Knoxville.

17. There is one area where Europe could learn from America. New innovative waste-treatment technologies, such as the plasma arc chamber, molten-salt incinerators, and transportable treatment units (TTUs), could be the American wave of the future, providing needed treatment capacity to complement the passion for waste reduction. This type of waste disposal is especially needed by those firms that cannot afford the capital expenditures for on-site change, but can afford to lease transportable treatment equipment. Government should assist in testing of TTUs, since they represent a simple change in tactics that solves many of today's roadblocks to effective treatment of toxics. By bringing the treatment equipment directly to the waste—rather than shipping the wastes to the equipment—the many risks of packaging and transport are avoided. By helping to define new priorities in treatment options, they may restore public confidence in business's ability to treat its own wastes. On top of that, TTUs

avoid one of the touchiest problems of hazardous-waste treatment: siting a fixed treatment facility.
18. Boulder, Colorado: Shambhala, 1979.

CHAPTER 6

1. We feel that most critics of environmentalism are victims of "false correctness." They condemn the movement for its incorrectness, but miss the message: survival, and an upgrading of physical and mental comfort. Since most of the critics of the movement typecast environmentalists in too simple a fashion, it is our purpose to display the immense variety the movement contains. In this way, our essay attempts to correct the "false correctness" of the movement's many critics.
2. For a vivid account of the story of Love Canal and its many sister sites, see Michael Brown's groundbreaking *Laying Waste: The Poisoning of America by Toxic Chemicals* (New York: Pantheon, 1979). Brown was there as Lois Gibbs discovered her plight. For those who desire more than history, see Brown's more recent book on the atmospheric transport of pollution, *The Toxic Cloud* (New York: Pantheon, 1986).
3. In a March 27, 1989, article in *The Nation,* Dick Russell reported that the groundswell of concern about the environment offered a new challenge to the various factions within the environmental movement. He observed: "a tension between the increasingly militant grass roots and the environmental establishment in Washington threatens to divide the movement. The mainstream conservation organizations believe they are at last about to see a serious governmental commitment to saving the environment. But many local groups fear, with some cause, that the well-heeled organizations lobbying in Washington are too ready to compromise with both governmental agencies and corporate polluters."
4. When Piasecki and research assistant Monica Smith met with Gibbs at her office, they were rapidly disabused of the impressions they had received in a set of briefings from state and federal officials. Most had misunderstood her. Neither devil nor angel, Lois is so down-to-earth you can feel it beneath your feet as she talks. Along with this earthiness, Lois has an impeccable understanding of the power of the media. "The media is more democratic than legislation," she told us, adding that "in the arena of public opinion, democracy works." On the issue of risk-assessment disputes, she commented astutely: "There is only political science, not good science. That's because science is funded for political reasons."
5. Kaufmann is the type of government worker who takes the oath of public service seriously. Another government whistle-blower of note, one who has earned the distinction of outlasting his in-house agency critics, is Felix Smith. He was supposed to retire three years ago from his California U.S. Fish and Wildlife post. His continued refusal to stop releasing embarrassing details about how his employer, the federal government, was misrepresenting the extent of selenium poisoning at the Kesterson National Wildlife Refuge in California drew the wrath of numerous officials who have either retired or been fired, demoted, or transferred to other assignments.

   He had agreed, after persistent harassment, that he would leave his post on January 7, 1987. This arrangement had been carefully crafted by superiors who hoped the troublesome Smith would disappear into the black hole of retirement. Members of Congress, environmentalists, and even fellow bureaucrats, however, advised him that the attempt to ouster him could not be enforced. Today he continues to fight, "trying to bring some balance to water resource development and fish and wildlife interests."

Smith's troubles stem from his actions in 1984, when he issued to the press an unauthorized account of the environmental contamination at Kesterson. He has, since then, also questioned the impacts of the Bureau of Reclamation's immense water projects, being an early advocate of what has come to be known as the public trust doctrine. This doctrine holds that all fish, wildlife, recreation, and navigation resources should be protected by government. The California State Supreme Court validated Smith's legal outlook when it restricted diversions from Mono Lake to Los Angeles in 1988, proving that Smith, and not his agency superiors, had envisioned the proper relationship between resource protection and use.

6. For detailed analyses on the role of watchdog groups, see Piasecki and Gary Davis, *Beyond Dumping* (Westport, Conn.: Greenwood Press, 1984), chapter 4; and *America's Future in Toxic Waste Management: Lessons from Europe* (Westport, Conn.: Greenwood Press, 1988), chapter 9.

7. As noted in the prologue, ocean incineration first brought Bruce Piasecki and Peter Asmus together. While Piasecki was finishing *America's Future,* Asmus was working on news stories on ocean incineration funded by a grant from the Northern California Fund for Investigative Journalism. The first full-length story, which ran in the October 18, 1987, issue of the *Sacramento Bee*'s "Forum" section, was then republished in different forms in *Los Angeles Herald-Examiner, Los Angeles Daily Journal, Long Beach Press Telegram,* and *Oakland Tribune.* Another article, for the March/April 1988 *Greenpeace* magazine, again featured Piasecki's research on Europe and came out just as the EPA finally abandoned attempts at continuing the ocean incineration burn program.

8. Dick Russell, in *The Nation,* March 27, 1989, reported that issues such as the Deep South's "cancer alley" are stimulating militant environmental protests by those frustrated with the slow pace of courtroom proceedings. For instance, shortly after the November 1988 elections, hundreds of people marched along the eighty-mile expanse of "cancer alley"—which runs from Baton Rouge to New Orleans—protesting the health consequences of toxic contamination from the 136 petrochemical and industrial plants in the region.

Militant acts can lead to new notions of justice, Russell observes. In July 1988, five South Carolina citizens who were arrested for blocking trucks from dumping chemicals into local drinking-water supplies were acquitted of civil disobedience charges. The Sumter County jury's acceptance of their plea of self-defense was the first time such a tactic had been successfully employed since 1974, when Sam Lovejoy was acquitted for environmental sabotage. The 1974 acquittal has been credited with vitalizing the antinuclear movement.

9. *America's Future in Toxic Waste Management,* by Piasecki and Gary Davis, explores several hundred of these safer alternatives.

10. As of this writing, the Federal Bureau of Investigation just filed a suit against three members of Earth First! in Phoenix, Arizona, for allegedly attempting to penetrate the Palo Verde nuclear plant. According to two prosecuting attorneys assembling the case, their "intent" was to cause a meltdown.

11. This comment by Dave Foreman was made on January 25, 1988, before an international conference entitled "Restoring the Earth" on the University of California–Berkeley campus. Foreman has repeated it many times since.

12. Students of animal behavior know that, when confronted with fire, all antelope follow their designated pathfinder. It's startling, this natural pulling into rank and order when emergencies arrive. Do humans lack a similar instinct?

13. For a detailed legal analysis of the shortsightedness of this approach, and a fuller

explanation of a more productive alternative now available in federal law, please see Piasecki's "Extinguishing Hazardous Waste Liabilities: New Strategies and Old Fallacies" in *Houston Law Review,* vol. 25, no. 4 (July 1988), pp. 855–76. In fact, those interested in the law community's awareness of the problem should read this entire *HLR* issue, devoted to waste liabilities.

14. Some scholars, such as Daniel Farber, Henry Fletcher Professor of Law at the University of Minnesota, claim that we "need to stop trying to ban pollution and start letting corporations pay for the privilege of polluting." Incentives have to be developed, he postulates, to turn pollution into a business cost that a company will want to minimize just like any other cost, such as labor or materials. He argues that the expense of pollution controls—now estimated at $70 billion a year—could be cut in half by utilizing new approaches such as emission fees and pollution permits. He notes that the EPA is making some moves in this direction and has already saved $500 million to $700 million in enforcement costs without any corresponding drop in environmental quality.

15. Whereas Tucker and Brown represent divergent approaches to environmental reform, Leo Marx, the well-known author of *The Machine in the Garden: Technology and the Pastoral Ideal in America,* sees such contradictions as natural outgrowths of the evolution of mankind's relationship with nature. He notes that the tension inherent in embracing technological progress and the pastoral ideals associated with natural resources has created institutional and cultural roadblocks to defining a coherent policy on the environment. According to Marx, Americans have simultaneous urges for two kingdoms—the machine and the garden—and the struggle between these two notions has extracted a heavy toll on contemporary politics, institutions, and technologies. The result? Strange juxtapositions. Though three-quarters of the American population label themselves environmentalists, for example, a good number of these professed nature lovers drive polluting cars over long commute distances to and from suburbs created by the deformation of wilderness landscapes.

16. We use the phrase "thieves and vagabonds" quite deliberately. The terms in which "troublesome radical activists" are described by critics are often so exaggerated that it would seem as if there never had been a hypocrite, a tyrant, a traitor, a faked virtue, or a convenient crime before there were radical environmentalists. By stepping back, and by adding a glimmer of historical distance to this chapter, we hope to more generously and more accurately describe these "fringe elements" in a future book.

17. Southern California's Zond Systems Wind Development Company witnessed firsthand the obstacles facing renewable energy projects. The objections came from environmental groups. After investing more than $1 million in a planned 77-megawatt wind energy project that would have served the energy needs of an estimated 25,000 homes, Zond was dismayed to learn that the Sierra Club and the Audubon Society joined up with a major local land developer (who was worried about the impact of such a project on nearby subdivisions) to deny a development permit. Both of these groups support wind energy in their national charter.

To Zond's dismay, the local Sierra Club, which gave the project a green light, had been overruled by state Sierra Club officials. Audubon claimed its opposition stemmed from concerns about California condors possibly running into the windmills, a fear which Zond claimed was irrational. After all, the chances of running into power poles and radio towers had not stopped construction of these structures.

Given that this would have been the first wind project in the Los Angeles area—home to the nation's worst air—this rejection illustrates how environmentalists can sometimes be part of the problem. "Our wind farm will generate energy and reduce air pollution," complained Zond's Jim Dehlsen, chairman of the firm. "The public knows that and they can't understand why a simple wind park can't go forward in Los Angeles."

18. Hollywood's conversion to the cause of the environment is not without its drawbacks, as Tinseltown is, of course, filled with its share of thieves and vagabonds. When Chico Mendes, the Brazilian activist, was brutally assassinated because of his efforts to preserve the rain forest for his fellow rubber tappers, Hollywood rushed to appear at the side of his widow, Ilza. Folks as diverse as Ted Turner, Robert Redford, and William Shatner looked at this story.

Eventually, close to a dozen filmmakers traversed the jungles of Brazil to seal a deal, but they were frustrated. Some observers lobbied against any film, because of concerns about the environmental impact of Hollywood forces invading the delicate jungles of Brazil. The widowed Ilza Mendes finally decided to award the rights to an obscure Brazilian company, but the rubber tappers disavowed the decision. Turner and Redford have pledged to proceed on their own.

19. Logic may be clean; science may be, at times, clear-cut. But environmental answers must be, above all else, based on notions of common sense that help us manage. We are not suggesting that technical reason should be stifled, or scientific eloquence gagged. Quite the opposite is our intent. But every person who has developed an environmental answer knows that nothing is so useless as a general maxim of science, or a legal precedent, when the basis of the decision rests on managerial common sense.

20. Readers may find it ironic that we cite the termination of Chemical Waste Management's proposal for ocean incineration off the Texas coast as an example of a great victory, and then proceed to quote a CWM spokesman talking about the environment. We include the views of a George Vander Velde in order to broaden the definition of *environmentalist* to include the full spectrum of people who will be shaping answers to environmental woes. Saving the environment is not just the job of rich professionals from New York, government whistle-blowers such as Hugh Kaufmann, or even working-class heroes such as Lois Gibbs. Saving the environment is also a calling for corporations that are creating a profit center by cleaning up past mistakes and preventing future ones.

21. A study released by the EPA in March 1989 revealed that air quality in the United States was at least three times worse than previously believed. The EPA found that approximately 2.4 billion pounds of toxic chemicals are spewed into the air annually by industrial sources alone, including sixty different cancer-causing substances. Additionally, the EPA reported that more than one hundred million U.S. citizens live in areas that fail to meet federal air-quality standards. Recent seasonal warming trends resulted in a fourteen-percent jump in ozone levels between 1987 and 1988.

About the Authors

Bruce W. Piasecki is the founder and president of the American Hazard Control Group, based in Castleton-on-the-Hudson, New York. The AHC Group provides legal, planning, and communications advice on environmental management decisions. In addition, Dr. Piasecki is a professor at Rensselaer Polytechnic Institute's Center for Urban and Environmental Studies in Troy, New York, with a joint appointment in their School of Management and MBA program.

Dr. Piasecki has been a contractor with several state and federal governments, including the New York State Energy Research and Development Authority, the New Jersey Hazardous Waste Facilities Siting Commission, and the Ontario Waste Management Corporation. Internationally, he has been a recipient of various grants, including the German Marshall Fund of the United States, for his research throughout Europe on environmental management developments. Coauthor (with Gary Davis) of *America's Future in Toxic Waste Management: Lessons from Europe* (1988) and *Beyond Dumping* (1984), he received his BA and PhD from Cornell University.

Peter Asmus is assistant editor of *California Policy Choices,* published by the University of Southern California School of Public Administration, and reports regularly on energy issues for McGraw-Hill's *Electric Utility Week, Independent Power Report,* and *Industrial User Bulletin.* Asmus is also a Sacramento correspondent for the *California Energy Markets* newsletter. Articles have appeared in *The Christian Science Monitor, Greenpeace* magazine, *Los Angeles Times, Sacramento Bee,* and *San Jose Mercury News,* among others. His consulting clients include Consumers Union, the Center for Investigative Reporting, and USC's Citizen Research Foundation.

HONORABLE ROBERT K. DAWSON

From 1987 through 1989, Bob Dawson was associate director of the U.S. Office of Management and Budget responsible specifically for energy, natural resources, and science. In this role, he had responsibility for forty percent of the annual budget of the United States for programs assigned to the Agriculture, Energy, and Interior departments; NASA, EPA, TVA, the U.S. Army Corps of Engineers, CEQ, NRC, Smithsonian Institution, Office of Science and Technology Policy, Woodrow Wilson International Center for Scholars, and the National Gallery of Art.

Earlier he had been appointed by President Reagan as deputy assistant secretary of the army for civil works, and in 1984 assumed the post of assistant secretary of the army for civil works responsible for Corps of Engineers civil works, overseas-nation building programs, and Panama Canal Commission activities.

Mr. Dawson is now vice president of management at Cassidy and Associates in Washington, D.C.

CONGRESSWOMAN CLAUDINE SCHNEIDER

A member of Congress for several sessions, Claudine Schneider is co-chair of the Congressional Competitiveness Caucus and vice chair of the Subcommittee on Natural Resources, Agriculture Research and Environment of the House Committee on Science, Space and Technology.

JEAN-MICHEL COUSTEAU

Jean-Michel Cousteau is director of many of the Cousteau Society's worldwide films, research projects, and reports.